AMERICAN ESSAYS IN ... SERIES

Series Editor, Edward Foley

THE
BYZANTINE RITE

A Short History

Robert F. Taft, S.J.

A Liturgical Press Book

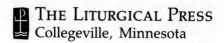

THE LITURGICAL PRESS
Collegeville, Minnesota

6   7   8   9

Library of Congress Cataloging-in-Publication Data

Taft, Robert F.
    The Byzantine rite : a short history / Robert F. Taft.
        p.   cm. — (American essays in liturgy)
    Includes bibliographical references.
    ISBN 0-8146-2163-5
    1. Orthodox Church—Byzantine rite—History.   I. Title.
    II. Series: American essays in liturgy (Collegeville, Minn.)
    BX4711.12.T34   1992
    264'.015—dc20   92-32645
                                                        CIP

To Mary Kerby,
for liking what I write.

Contents

Abbreviations

AL = Analecta Liturgica.

ANTF = Arbeiten zur neutestamentlichen Forschung.

AOC = Archives de l'Orient chrétien.

Arranz, "Hesperinos" = M. Arranz, "L'office de l'Asmatikos Hesperinos ('vêpres chantées') de l'ancien Euchologe byzantin," OCP 44 (1978) 107–130, 391–412.

Arranz, "Étapes" = id., "Les grandes étapes de la Liturgie Byzantine: Palestine-Byzance-Russie. Essai d'aperçu historique," in *Liturgie de l'église particulière, liturgie de l'église universelle*, BELS 7 (Rome 1976) 43–72.

Arranz, "Euchologe slave" = id., "La liturgie de l'Euchologe slave du Sinai," in *Christianity among the Slavs. The Heritage of Saints Cyril and Methodius*. Acts of the International Congress held on the Eleventh Centenary of the Death of St. Methodius, Rome, October 8–11, 1985, under the direction of the Pontifical Oriental Institute. Edited by Edward C. Farrugia, S.J., Robert F. Taft, S.J., Gino K. Piovesana, S.J., with the Editorial Committee, OCA 231 (Rome 1988) 15–74.

Arranz, "Matines" = id., "Les prières presbytérales des matines byzantines," OCP 37 (1971) 406–436, 38 (1972) 64–115.

Arranz, "Sacrements," I = id., "Les sacrements de l'ancien Euchologe constantinopolitain," 1: OCP 48 (1982) 284–335; 2: 49 (1983) 42–90; 3: 49 (1983) 284–302; 4: 50 (1984) 43–64; 5: 50 (1984) 372–397; 6: 51 (1985) 60–86; 7: 52 (1986) 145–178; 8: 53 (1987) 59–106; 9: 55 (1989) 33–62; "La consécration du saint myron" (= "Sacrements" I.10) 55 (1989) 317–338.

Arranz, "Sacrements," II = id., "Les sacrements de la restauration de l'ancien Euchologe constantinopolitain," 1: OCP 56 (1990) 283–322; 2.1: 57 (1991) 87–143; 2.2: 57 (1991) 309–329; 2.3: 58 (1992) 23–82 (continuing).

Arranz, "Sacrements," III = id., "Les sacrements de l'institution de l'ancien Euchologe constantinopolitain," 1: OCP 56 (1990) 83–133 (continuing).

Arranz, *Typicon* = id. (ed.), *Le Typicon du Monastère du Saint-Sauveur à Messine. Codex Messinensis gr. 115, AD 1131*, OCA 185 (Rome 1969).

Baldovin = J. F. Baldovin, *The Urban Character of Christian Worship. The Origins, Development, and Meaning of Stational Liturgy*, OCA 228 (Rome 1987).

BELS = Bibliotheca *Ephemerides Liturgicae* Subsidia.

BSGRT = Bibliotheca Scriptorum Graecorum et Romanorum Teubneriana (Leipzig).

CA = *Cahiers archéologiques*

Conomos, *Communion Cycle* = D. E. Conomos, *The Late Byzantine and Slavonic Communion Cycle: Liturgy and Music* (Washington 1985).

CPG = *Clavis patrum Graecorum* I-V, ed. M. Geerard, F. Glorie, Corpus Christianorum (Turnhout 1983–1987).

CSHB = Corpus scriptorum historiae Byzantinae.

Dagron, "Les moines" = G. Dagron, "Les moines de la ville. Le monachisme à Constantinople jusqu'au concile de Chalcédoine (451)," *Travaux et mémoires* 4 (1970) 229–276.

Dmitrievskij I, II, III = A. Dmitrievskij, *Opisanie liturgicheskix rukopisej xranjashchixsja v bibliotekax pravoslavnago vostoka*, I-II (Kiev 1895, 1901); III (Petrograd 1917).

DOP = *Dumbarton Oaks Papers.*

GCS = Die griechischen christlichen Schriftsteller der ersten drei Jahrhunderte.

Jacob, "Tradition" = A. Jacob, "La tradition manuscrite de la Liturgie de S. Jean Chrysostome (VIIIe–XIIe siècles)," in *Eucharisties d'Orient et d'Occident* 2, Lex orandi 47 (Paris 1970) 109–138.

JöB = *Jahrbuch der österreichischen Byzantinistik.*

JTS = *The Journal of Theological Studies.*

Kähler = H. Kähler, *Hagia Sophia*, with a chapter on the Mosaics by Cyril Mango (New York/Washington 1967).

LEW = F. E. Brightman, *Liturgies Eastern and Western* (Oxford 1896).

Mango, *Architecture* = C. Mango, *Byzantine Architecture*, History of World Architecture (New York 1976).

Mango, *Art* = id., *The Art of the Byzantine Empire, 312-1453,* Sources and Documents in the History of Art Series (Englewood Cliffs, N.J. 1972).

Mango, "Daily Life" = id., "Daily Life in Byzantium," JöB 31.1 (1981) 337-353; "Addendum to the Report on Everyday Life," JöB 32.1 (1982) 252-257.

Mango, *Materials* = id., *Materials for the Study of the Mosaics of St. Sophia at Istanbul,* Dumbarton Oaks Studies 7 (Washington 1961).

Mango, "Mosaics" = id., "The Mosaics of Hagia Sophia," Chapter VIII in Kähler 47-60.

Mateos, *Célébration* = J. Mateos, *La célébration de la parole dans la liturgie byzantine,* OCA 191 (Rome 1971).

Mateos, *Typicon* I-II = id. (ed.), *Le Typicon de la Grande Église. Ms. Sainte-Croix no. 40, Xe siècle. Introduction, texte critique, traduction et notes,* 2 vols., OCA 165-166 (Rome 1962-1963).

Mathews = T. F. Mathews, *The Early Churches of Constantinople: Architecture and Liturgy* (University Park, Penn./London 1971).

P. Meyendorff, *Germanus* = *St. Germanus of Constantinople on the Divine Liturgy,* The Greek text with translation, introduction, and commentary by Paul Meyendorff (Crestwood, N.Y. 1984).

MMB = Monumenta Musicae Byzantinae.

Nicol = D. M. Nicol, *Church and Society in the Last Centuries of Byzantium* (Cambridge 1979).

OC = *Oriens Christianus.*

OCA = Orientalia Christiana Analecta.

OCP = *Orientalia Christiana Periodica.*

ODB = *The Oxford Dictionary of Byzantium,* 3 vols., ed. Alexander P. Kazhdan, with A.-M. Talbot, A. Cutler, T. E. Gregory, N. Ševčenko (New York/Oxford 1991).

Parenti, *Gb IV* = S. Parenti, *L'Eucologio manoscritto Gb IV (X secolo) della Biblioteca di Grottaferrata. Edizione* (doctoral dissertation in preparation at the Pontifical Oriental Institute under the direction of Miguel Arranz, S.J.).

Parenti, "Influssi" = id., "Influssi italo-greci nei testi eucaristici bizantini dei 'Fogli Slavi' del Sinai (XI sec.)," OCP 57 (1991) 145-177.

Parenti, "Osservazioni" = id., "Osservazioni sul testo dell'Anafora di Giovanni Crisostomo in alcuni eucologi italo-greci (VIII–XI secolo)," *Ephemerides Liturgicae* 105 (1991) 120–154.

SA = Studia Anselmiana.

Schulz = H.-J. Schulz, *The Byzantine Liturgy. Symbolic Structure and Faith Expression* (New York 1986).

Strunk, *Music* = O. Strunk, *Essays on Music in the Byzantine World* (New York 1977).

Taft, *Beyond East and West* = R. F. Taft, *Beyond East and West. Problems in Liturgical Understanding* (Washington 1984).

Taft, "Bibliography" = id., "Select Bibliography on the Byzantine Liturgy of the Hours," OCP 48 (1982) 358–370.

Taft, *Great Entrance* = id., *The Great Entrance. A History of the Transfer of Gifts and Other Preanaphoral Rites of the Liturgy of St. John Chrysostom*, OCA 200, 2nd ed. (Rome 1978).

Taft, *Hours* = id., *The Liturgy of the Hours in East and West. The Origins of the Divine Office and its Meaning for Today* (Collegeville 1986).

Taft, "Liturgy" = id., "The Liturgy of the Great Church: An Initial Synthesis of Structure and Interpretation on the Eve of Iconoclasm," DOP 34/35 (1980–1981) 45–75.

Taft, "Mt. Athos" = id., "Mount Athos: A Late Chapter in the History of the Byzantine Rite," DOP 42 (1988) 179–194.

Taft, "Paschal Triduum" = id., "In the Bridegroom's Absence. The Paschal Triduum in the Byzantine Church," in *La celebrazione del Triduo pasquale: anamnesis e mimesis*, Atti del III Congresso Internazionale di Liturgia, Roma, Pontificio Istituto Liturgico, 9–13 maggio 1988, AL 14 = SA 102 (Rome 1990) 71–97.

Taft, "A Tale of Two Cities" = id., "A Tale of Two Cities. The Byzantine Holy Week Triduum as a Paradigm of Liturgical History," in J. Neil Alexander (ed.), *Time and Community, in Honor of Thomas Julian Talley*, NPM Studies in Church Music and Liturgy (Washington 1990) 21–41.

Thiermeyer, *Ottoboni gr. 434* = A.-A. Thiermeyer, *Das Euchologion Ottoboni gr. 434* (doctoral dissertation under my direction at the Pontifical Oriental Institute, Rome 1992).

TU = Texte und Untersuchungen.

Vogt, texte I-II; commentaire I-II = A. Vogt (ed.), *Le Livre des cérémonies de Constantin Porphyrogénète*, texte I–II (Paris 1935, 1939); commentaire I–II (Paris 1935, 1940).

Introduction

Introduction

Almost forty years ago and a decade before the promulgation of the Vatican II *Constitution on the Sacred Liturgy*—the "Magna Charta" of modern Catholic liturgy—The Liturgical Press of Collegeville published *A Brief History of Liturgy* by the late Professor Theodore Klauser (1894–1984) of the University of Bonn. As was customary in those sometimes myopic pre-Vatican II days, the title of this brief pamphlet had it wrong. Klauser's essay was not about *liturgy*, but about *western liturgy*; and not even about all of that, but only about western *Catholic* liturgy. To be fair, Dr. Klauser may not have been responsible for that title. His 1953 The Liturgical Press pamphlet was actually a résumé of his book-length study, more accurately entitled *A Short History of the Western Liturgy*, which first appeared in German in 1943. The enormous success of Klauser's history—it went through at least five German editions and three English editions (1969, 1973, and 1979)—is sufficient proof of the need it has filled.

Unfortunately, oriental liturgiologists have not yet been able to provide a similar overview of the history of the most important and most studied eastern liturgical tradition, the Byzantine. If a certain number of extremely valuable studies on Byzantine liturgical theology or mystagogy have appeared recently,[1] and if there is almost an *embarras de richesses* on Byzantine architecture and iconography, including church decorative programs,[2] we are less well provided with reliable attempts to delineate the entire historical evolution of what Alexander Schmemann called "the Byzantine synthesis."[3] Schmemann himself attempted such an historical overview in his still popular *Introduction to Liturgical Theology*. Fresher outlines of this synthesis are now available,[4] and the following pages will present what I think can be said about this question at the present stage of research in a field where much is unknown, a great deal is hypothetical, and an enormous amount of work remains to be done. It will not be possible to write the full history of Byzantine liturgical ritual until we have: more primary liturgical manuscripts edited critically and accompanied by serious commentaries situating them in their liturgical and historical context; more scholarly studies of the relevant liturgico-canonical material from the synods and councils with the same contextualization; more scholarly studies of Byzantine church music not just as musicology but from the point of view of its place in the history of the liturgy;[5] and a taxonomy or typology of the medieval liturgical books of the sort already available for the West.[6] For a full picture of the Byzantine Rite, however, not even that will suffice. The "Byzantine synthesis" comprises much more than just ritual, as we shall see.

In spite of this complexity, we do know something about the origins and evolution of this tradition—indeed, much more than we knew a generation ago. On the basis of the present state of our knowledge, I shall try to follow in the footsteps of Theodore Klauser with my own *kleine byzantinische Liturgiegeschichte*.

Note, however, that I do not intend to provide here a primer, nor even a description of Byzantine liturgy. Together with my colleagues at the Pontifical Oriental Institute in Rome, Professors Juan Mateos, S.J.,[7] and Miguel Arranz, S.J.,[8] I have already done that elsewhere, in more or less popular form,[9] as well as in numerous particular studies of a far more technical stamp.[10] Nor do I intend here a complete history of the Byzantine Rite from its origins up to the present. My aim, rather, is to trace the origins of this tradition during its period of formation: roughly speaking, from its earliest recorded beginnings until the end of Byzantium. The history of the Byzantine Rite, of course, did not end with the fall of Constantinople in 1453. Nor did Byzantine liturgical creativity come to a halt at that point. But by that time the Byzantine Rite had developed the

13

lineaments it has retained until today, and later developments do not alter this substance.

Rome, Pontifical Oriental Institute 1 January 1992, the Feast of the Circumcision and of St. Basil the Great according to the Byzantine Calendar.

Notes

1. State of the question and relevant literature in Taft, "Liturgy." See esp. R. Bornert, *Les commentaires byzantins de la Divine Liturgie du VIIe au XVe siècle*, AOC 9 (Paris 1966), and Schulz.

2. The relevant studies I have found most useful will be cited in the course of the following pages.

3. *Introduction to Liturgical Theology*, The Library of Orthodox Theology 4 (London/Portland, Me. 1966) ch. 4.

4. Arranz, "Étapes;" Taft, "Mt. Athos."

5. In this regard see the remarks in my review of Conomos, *Communion Cycle*, in *Worship* 62 (1988) 554–557.

6. C. Vogel, trans. and revised by W. Story and N. Rasmussen, *Medieval Liturgy. An Introduction to the Sources*, NPM Studies in Church Music and Liturgy (Washington 1986); E. Foley, "The *libri ordinarii:* An Introduction," *Ephemerides Liturgicae* 102 (1988) 129–137; and most recently, A.-G. Martimort, *Les "Ordines," les Ordinaires et les Cérémoniaux*, Typologie des sources du Moyen-âge occidental, Fasc. 56 = A-VI.A.1* (Louvain-la-Neuve 1991): the inside cover of this collection presents a succinct definition of the nature, purpose, and necessity of a typology of sources.

7. Especially *Célébration.*

8. Numerous studies on the Liturgy of the Hours, the sacraments, the Euchology and Horologion, the Typika, principally his over 30 articles in OCP 37 (1971) up to the present, many of which are listed in the "Abbreviations" at the beginning of this volume, or in Taft, "Bibliography," nos. 29–30, 49–61, 157; id., "Mt. Athos," 180 no. 7.

9. R. Taft, *Eastern-Rite Catholicism. Its Heritage and Vocation*, Paulist Press Doctrinal Pamphlet Series (Glen Rock, N.J. 1963; reprinted N.Y., John XXIII Ecumenical Center, Fordham University 1976, 1978; Center for Eastern Christian Studies, University of Scranton 1988); *Beyond East and West*, chs. 3, 4, 8, 9, 11; "Russian Liturgy, a Mirror of the Russian Soul," in *Studi albanologici, balcanici, bizantini e orientali in onore di Giuseppe Valentini, S.J.*, Studi albanesi, Studi e testi VI (Flor-

ence 1986) 413–435; "Liturgy and Eucharist. I. East," ch. 18 of Jill Raitt (ed.), *Christian Spirituality: High Middle Ages and Reformation,* vol. 17 of *World Spirituality: An Encyclopedic History of the Religious Quest* (N.Y. 1987) 415–426.

10. In addition to numerous articles in OCP from 35 (1969) to the present, see especially: *Great Entrance; Hours,* 48, 171–174, and ch. 17; *A History of the Liturgy of St. John Chrysostom,* vol. IV: *The Diptychs,* OCA 238 (Rome 1991); "Psalm 24 at the Transfer of Gifts in the Byzantine Liturgy: a Study in the Origins of a Liturgical Practice," in R. J. Clifford and G. W. MacRae (eds.), *The Word in the World,* Essays in Honor of Frederick L. Moriarty, S.J., (Cambridge, Mass.: Weston College Press 1973) 159–177; "The Byzantine Divine Liturgy. History and Commentary," *Diakonia* 8 (1973) 164–178; "The Inclination Prayer before Communion in the Byzantine Liturgy of St. John Chrysostom: A Study in Comparative Liturgy," *Ecclesia orans* 3 (1986) 29–60; "Water into Wine. The Twice-Mixed Chalice in the Byzantine Eucharist," *Le Muséon* 100 (1987) 323–342; "Melismos and Comminution. The Fraction and its Symbolism in the Byzantine Tradition," in G. Farnedi (ed.), *Traditio et progressio. Studi liturgici in onore del Prof. Adrien Nocent, OSB,* AL 12 = SA 95 (Rome 1988) 531–552; "The Litany following the Anaphora in the Byzantine Liturgy," in W. Nyssen (ed.), *Simandron. Der Wachklopfer. Gedenkschrift für Klaus Gamber (1919–1989)* (Cologne 1989) 233–256; "Paschal Triduum"; "A Tale of Two Cities"; " 'Holy Things for the Saints.' The Ancient Call to Communion and its Response," in G. Austin (ed.) *Fountain of Life. In Memory of Niels K. Rasmussen, O.P.,* NPM Studies in Church Music and Liturgy (Washington 1991) 87–102; "The Fruits of Communion in the Anaphora of St. John Chrysostom," to appear in a *Festschrift* for Jordi Pinell, O.S.B., AL = SA (Rome, in press); and 95 articles on Byzantine liturgy in ODB.

1 The Byzantine Rite

What liturgists, for want of a more comprehensive and neutral term, call "the Byzantine Rite," is the liturgical system that developed in the Orthodox Patriarchate of Constantinople and was gradually adopted, in the Middle Ages, by the other Chalcedonian Orthodox Patriarchates of Alexandria, Antioch, and Jerusalem.[1] This Byzantine synthesis, by far the most widespread Eastern Christian liturgical heritage, is still used by all the Churches that derive from this Orthodox Pentarchy.

The Byzantine liturgical system, renowned for the sumptuousness of its ceremonial and liturgical symbolism, heritage of the imperial splendors of Constantinople before the eighth century, is actually a hybrid of Constantinopolitan and Palestinian rites, gradually synthesized during the ninth to the fourteenth centuries in the monasteries of the Orthodox world, beginning in the period of the struggle with Iconoclasm.[2]

Its Components

Like other traditional Christian liturgical families, the Byzantine Rite comprises the following: the "Divine Liturgy" (eucharist); the other "mysteries" (sacraments) of baptism, chrismation (confirmation), crowning (marriage), unction, penance, and ordination; matins, vespers, vigils and the other hours; the liturgical year with its calendar of fixed and movable cycles of feasts and fasts and saints' days; plus a variety of lesser services or *akolouthiai* (blessings, the consecration of a church, exorcisms, monastic investiture, etc.). All of these are codified in the standard anthologies or liturgical books of the tradition.

As in other traditions, Byzantine liturgical books are either liturgical texts actually used in the services, or are instructions that regulate how such texts are to be used. The texts themselves contain the customary two levels of elements: the *ordinary*, or basic, invariable skeleton of the offices; and the *proper*, that varies according to the feast or day. The Byzantine ordinary is contained in the Euchology or Prayerbook of prayers and litanies for the use of the celebrant and deacon, and the Horologion or Book of Hours. The seasonal propers of the *mobile cycle* that revolves around Easter are found in three books: the Triodion for Lent, the Pentekostarion for the Easter/Pentecost season, and the Oktoechos used on Sundays and weekdays throughout the year (except when it is replaced by the other two seasonal anthologies). The *fixed cycle* of propers for the sanctoral commemorations and feasts that fall on the 365 dates of the calendar year are found, one volume per month, in the twelve-volume Menaion or "monthly." The New Testament readings proper to both cycles are found in two lectionaries: the Apostle and the Gospel. The lections from the Old Testament, now read only in the Divine Office, have been incorporated into the other books of the proper. The Typikon, or book of rules, is the "customary" that regulates the use of these books according to the feasts and seasons of the Church year.

This dry, material description of the Byzantine Rite fails to manifest its poetic richness, its intensity, or its tightly-woven unity of ritual celebration, ritual setting, and ritual interpretation. Byzantine liturgy and its theology—within the native context of Byzantine church architecture, church decoration, and liturgical disposition which enfold the ritual like its natural womb—join to forge what H.-J. Schulz has felicitously called a peculiar *Symbolgestalt* or symbolic matrix.[3] The impact of this *Symbolgestalt* is forever enshrined in the legend of the delegation sent to Constantinople in 987 by Prince Vladimir of Kiev "to examine the Greek faith." The emissaries were led to Hagia Sophia for the liturgy, "so that the Russes might behold the glory of the God of the Greeks." On returning home they reported what they had experienced in terms that have become emblematic for the *Erscheinungsbild*,[4] or unique impact created by the sensible splendors of the Byzantine Rite:

> We knew not whether we were in heaven or on earth. For on earth there is no such splendor or such beauty, and we are at a loss how to describe it. We know only that God dwells there among men, and their service is fairer than the ceremonies of other nations. For we cannot forget that beauty.[5]

"Heaven on earth." This classic phrase, repeated so often it has become a topos, actually derives from the opening chapter of the earlier liturgical commentary (ca. 730) of Patriarch St. Germanus I of Constantinople: "The church is heaven on earth, where the God of heaven dwells and moves."[6]

Less easily discernable than the provenance of the topos, however, is the exceedingly intricate history of what provoked this classic reaction in the first place: not just the Byzantine liturgical system, but the architectural and decorative system devised to enclose it, as well as the mystagogy that explains it. I insist on all three, for the Byzantine synthesis is not just the first element, ritual celebration in a vacuum. As H.-J. Schulz has demonstrated in his excellent study of the Byzantine eucharist, one of the distinguishing characteristics of the Byzantine Rite is precisely its intimate symbiosis of liturgical symbolism (ritual celebration), liturgical setting (architecture/iconography), and liturgical interpretation (mystagogy).[7] Any true history of the Byzantine Rite must account for their interaction in the evolution of the tradition.

Historical Phases

I divide the history of this Byzantine liturgical synthesis into five, sometimes overlapping phases:[8]

1. the paleo-Byzantine or pre-Constantinian era, about which we know little;

2. the "imperial phase" during the Late Antique or patristic period, especially from the reign of Justinian I (527–565) and his immediate successors, creating a system of cathedral liturgy that lasted until some time after the Latin Conquest (1204–1261), thus overlapping with phases 3–4;

18

3. the "Dark Ages" from 610 to ca. 850, and especially the struggle against Iconoclasm (726–843), culminating in the Studite reform;

4. the Studite era itself, from ca. 800–1204;

5. the final, neo-Sabaitic synthesis after the Latin conquest (1204–1261).

Phases 2–3, the most important for our purposes, will be the main focus of our interest here. During Phase 1, the liturgy of Byzantium was a typical Late Antique, Antiochene-type rite with no especially distinguishing traits. The same was apparently the case with the early churches of Constantinople: neither the shape nor the symbolism of the rite or its buildings were distinguishably "Byzantine." But in the last two decades of the fourth century, especially from the reign of Theodosius I (379–395), the rite of Constantinople began to acquire the stational character and theological lineaments that will mark its later history. Phase 4, covering (if not exactly coterminous with) the entire Middle-Byzantine Period, was dominated liturgically by the progress of the Studite synthesis—a monastic rite of quite different dimensions from the *Asmatike Akolouthia* or "Sung Office" of the cathedral rite of the Great Church. This monastic rite found its ultimate codification in the Studite Typika, which supplanted the cathedral rite of the Typikon of the Great Church in the restoration following 1261. As for Phase 5, though critical for the final neo-Sabaitic synthesis that gradually modified and ultimately supplanted the Studite Rite (itself an earlier generation "Sabaitic" rite) everywhere during the hesychast ascendancy,[9] it represents, basically, more of the same as far as the liturgy/church dynamic is concerned. I shall deal with this phase only *ad complementum doctrinae.*

I consider Phases 2–3 formative, not only of the Byzantine liturgy, but of the Byzantine liturgical vision, when the basis of what Schulz calls its *Erscheinungsbild* and *Symbolgestalt* emerged. This period was a time of formation, climax, breakdown, realignment, and new synthesis. It was a time in which changes in the shape and perception of the liturgy would, in the next, Middle-Byzantine Period[10] (our Phase 4), be mirrored by accompanying shifts in its architectural and iconographic setting. All these together are but a reflection of developments in church life and in the theology which itself is a meditation on that life. That, at least, is what I think the Byzantines themselves tell us in the extant sources.

Notes

1. Some writers prefer the term "Orthodox Liturgy," which is all right as far as it goes. But this term is not accurate enough to satisfy the liturgical scholar or historian. The Alexandrian Greek Liturgies of St. Mark or of St. Gregory, for example, are fully Orthodox liturgies—but by no stretch of the imagination are they Byzantine liturgies. Besides, several non-Byzantine Eastern Churches also call themselves "Orthodox."

2. This was an 8–9th c. heretical movement that opposed sacred images. It enjoyed official—that is, imperial—favor from 726–787, 815–843.

3. The term is from the German edition of Schulz.

4. Ibid.

5. S. H. Cross, O.P. Sherbowitz-Weltzor, *The Russian Primary Chronicle. Laurentian Text* (Cambridge, Mass. 1953) 110–111.

6. P. Meyendorff, *Germanus* 56 (my translation).

7. Schulz.

8. On the periodization of Byzantine history, see A. Kazhdan *et alii*, "Byzantium, History of," ODB 1:345–362. The traditional, albeit somewhat artificial and inadequate, threefold division into Early, Middle, and Late Byzantine Periods (the dates of which find no complete agreement among authors) is not very useful for the ecclesiastico-cultural history of which the liturgy was a prime expression. For our purposes a more useful division is: [1] the paleo-Byzantine period from 324 until Justinian (527); [2] the "Golden Age" of Justinian (527–565) and his immediate successors; [3] the "Dark Ages" from the mid-7th c. through the period of Iconoclasm (726–843), with the coming of St. Theodore and his monks to Stoudios in 799, and the final victory over Iconoclasm in 843, the key ecclesiastical landmarks; [4] the revival under the Macedonians and the Comnenoi from the 9th c. until the Fourth Crusade (1204); [5] the final Byzantine period from after the Latin conquest (1204–1261) and, for the Orthodox Church at least, continuing after the Fall of Constantinople to the Turks in 1453 into "Byzance après Byzance." In addition to the excellent summary of

Byzantine history in this ODB entry, see also D. G. Geanakoplos, *Byzantium. Church, Society, and Civilization Seen through Contemporary Eyes* (Chicago/London 1984) 1–13: ''Introduction: Byzantium's History in Outline.''

9. On the liturgical impact of hesychasm, a monastic movement of spiritual renewal in Orthodoxy from the 14th c. on, see Taft, ''Mt. Athos,'' 191–194, and the literature cited there.

10. See note 8 above.

2 Paleo-Byzantine Liturgy: Byzance avant Byzance

Modern Byzantinists have adopted the conceit of referring to the continued existence of Byzantine culture in Orthodox lands (Greece and Southern Italy, Romania, Serbia, Bulgaria, Kievan Rus', Muscovy, the Middle East) after the Fall of Constantinople in 1453 as "Byzance après Byzance." But there is also a sense in which one can speak of "Byzance avant Byzance." For, ironically, Byzantium did not become "Byzantine" in the modern sense of the term until it had been christened "Constantinople," leaving the original name of the city to designate the Medieval culture that Constantinople and its empire would produce.

When did the Byzantine Era begin? The Emperor Diocletian had divided the Roman Empire into East and West already in 293, but the split was made definitive only after the death of Theodosius I in 395. This is a date favored by some as the beginning of the Byzantine Era. Others hold that it is only in 476, when Odoacer deposed the last true western emperor (Romulus Augustulus) to become the first barbarian king of Italy (476–493) that the Byzantine Era began. At least by the reign of Justinian I (527–565), one can speak of the Byzantine Empire rather than the Roman Empire in the East. It is only under Justinian the Great that the liturgy of Constantinople became properly "Byzantine."

Byzantium becomes Constantinople

Of course, this is not when the history of the Byzantine liturgy began. Byzantium, an ancient Greek port town beauti-

fully and strategically situated on a peninsula overlooking the
Bosporus, had been in existence from at least the twelfth century B.C. It suddenly was catapulted into world prominence
in A.D. 324 when Emperor Constantine I (324–327) chose it as
his eastern capital. It was inaugurated as the capital a scant
six years later, on 11 May 330. There were Christians in the
city long before this period, however.

Like every town of any importance in Christian antiquity,
Byzantium was an episcopal see. Its bishops were suffragans
of the Metropolitan of Heraclea in Thrace within the Prefecture of Oriens. After Byzantium became Constantinople—the
New Rome—its see was promoted to second rank after Old
Rome at the First Council of Constantinople in 381. Canon 3
of that council declared that "The bishop of Constantinople
has the primacy of honor after the bishop of Rome, because
this city is the New Rome." This honorary primacy solidified
into something more substantial during the dynamic episcopate of John Chrysostom (398–404). Under his energetic
authority this honor began evolving into an effective primacy
of jurisdiction. Constantinople eventually carved out a patriarchate for itself by extending its jurisdiction over the (civil)
dioceses of Thrace in Europe, and Asia and Pontus in Asia
Minor. This *fait accompli* was recognized by canon 28 of the
Council of Chalcedon in 451.[1]

The Origins of the Liturgy in Byzantium

In a very real sense, one could locate the origins of the "Byzantine Church," as we know it, in the period from 381–451. It
is from this same period that we first hear of Constantinopolitan liturgy in the homilies of its bishops Gregory Nazianzen
(379–381), and especially John Chrysostom (398–404). From
these giants we learn something about vigils, stations and "litanies" (that is, the processions), preaching, psalmody and
chanting (both responsorial and the newly devised antiphonal),
and the eucharist.[2]

It is not surprising that the early Constantinopolitan eucharist (especially the anaphora) and the Cathedral Office of

the Great Church, seen in these and other extant remains, bear Antiochene traits. Byzantium was originally within the ecclesiastical zone dominated by the see of Antioch. This was the major center of liturgical diffusion within the Prefecture of Oriens.[3] In the pre-Constantinopolitan period, several bishops of Byzantium came from Antioch or its environs and participated in Antiochene synods. The greatest among them, John Chrysostom, was a presbyter in his native Antioch before becoming bishop of the capital in February 398. One of the things he brought from home and revised for use in his new episcopal see was the ancient Antiochene Anaphora of the Apostles, a prayer still used in the Byzantine Rite today as the Anaphora of St. John Chrysostom.[4]

The Formation of Rites

But this is still "Byzance avant Byzance": what I call the "paleo-Byzantine" phase of the history of the Byzantine Rite, when there was yet little properly "Byzantine" about the liturgical usages of New Rome. In this early period, when the liturgical families that were to emerge at the end of Late Antiquity were still in formation, one cannot yet speak of "rites" in the present sense of a coherent, unified corpus of liturgical usages followed by all churches within a single ecclesiastical conscription. This process of the unification of local liturgical usages into a single "rite" continued until the end of Late Antiquity.

Before the twentieth century the prevailing theory about the development of the various liturgical rites was what might be called the theory of "the diversification of rites." Formulated by the German scholar Ferdinand Probst,[5] this theory posited a primitive, apostolic liturgical unity that gradually evolved into distinct rites—much as the multitude of Indo-European languages developed out of the original parent language, Proto-Indoeuropean. There was some truth to this perspective; after all, there existed an original apostolic kerygma to which everything Christian can be ultimately traced.

Anton Baumstark (d. 1948), the famous German orientalist and liturgical scholar, finally put Probst's theory to rest in two seminal works.[6] As Baumstark demonstrated, the first three centuries of Christianity witnessed the development of a multitude of local liturgical uses. The period from the "Peace of Constantine" in 312 until the end of the first millennium was not one of greater liturgical diversification. Rather, as a result of the development of intermediate administrative church unities eventually called patriarchates, Christianity experienced an ongoing process of ritual unification within these distinct zones of ecclesiastical influence.

To continue our linguistic simile, in phase one the original kerygma, implanted in different areas, gave rise to a plethora of local liturgical usages. In a given region these usages were all of the same "type," just as Proto-Indoeuropean evolved into a multitude of eastern and western subfamilies,[7] each with its many dialects or spoken varieties even within the same limited geographical area. But in a later phase, the many *dialects* of each of these subgroups became unified into, or gave way before newer literary *languages*.[8] This process has not yet come to term. Even today, in a country as small as Italy, a wide variety of languages and dialects[9]—spinoffs from the débris of vulgar Latin—are still spoken in addition to "standard Italian." "Standard Italian" was originally but one of the dialects (Tuscan) that became the literary language because of the vagaries of history. Because there is an Italy, with a growing cultural unity within the country, more and more of the local dialects will die out and standardized Italian will eventually prevail. More and more Italians will hear and speak "Italian," not just at school, in parliament, at work, and on the radio and television, but also at home, on the street, and in the bar.

This last phase of linguistic development is similar to what happened to liturgies after the fourth century, as a multitude of related but different liturgical "dialects" within a given zone of ecclesiastical politico-cultural influence gave way to the growing predominance of the "standard" language or rite—usually that of the metropolis. The result was greater unity, not greater diversity. People speak fewer languages today than they once did. And beginning with the fourth century, they gradually came to celebrate in fewer and fewer liturgical rites.

The Emergence of the Byzantine Rite

We can reconstruct this process only from its extant monuments, and they represent but a few sporadic footprints left from a long trek. For Constantinople, at least, the extremities of the journey—its beginning and end—are clear enough. At the beginning of the fifth century, the liturgy of Constantinople was nothing but that. Archaeological and textual evidence from Greece, Cappadocia, and Pontus shows that the churches in these regions, even if under the political domination of the capital, did not use the same rite. But soon they began to adopt the same rite from the capital. By the end of the first millennium, the rite of the Great Church of Constantinople had spread far and wide. We have explicit proof from the eleventh century that it was used in Asia Minor.[10] It was also employed in other areas of the world under Byzantine influence during that period, as demonstrated by the extant Byzantine liturgical documents from the length and breadth of the empire: from Constantinople to Mt. Athos, Greece, Magna Graecia, Antiochia, Palestine, and Sinai.[11]

Our earliest extant Byzantine liturgical text, the beautiful uncial codex *Barberini 336* in the Vatican Library, dates from the middle of the eighth century. A century earlier, in 691–692, the liturgical canons of the Quinisext Council "in Trullo" show that the Byzantine Rite had already become cohesive and coherent enough to manifest its intolerance for the different practices of the Latins and the Armenians. Generally speaking, therefore, by the seventh century the multifarious rituals within a particular zone of ecclesiastico-cultural influence and authority had taken on recognizable form as a liturgical family or "rite" with characteristics that distinguished it from others.

This was only the beginning of a long process. The Byzantine Rite began, but did not end, with the unification of the "Rite of the Great Church" of Constantinople—especially of its cathedral, Hagia Sophia—by about the end of the seventh century. The rite of Constantinople then entered into a marriage of convenience with its most powerful neighboring tradition, the rite of Jerusalem, just as the rite of Old Rome would wed itself to that of Gaul. Before turning to that next phase of our history, let us take a closer look at some of the crucial developments that took place under Emperor Justinian the Great.

Notes

1. On the rise of Constantinople see H.-G. Beck, "Constantinople: The Rise of a New capital in the East," in K. Weitzmann (ed.), *Age of Spirituality: A symposium* (N.Y./Princeton 1980) 29–37; cf. Dagron, "Les moines," 276.

2. Taft, *Hours* 48, 171–174; F. van de Paverd, *Zur Geschichte der Meßliturgie in Antiocheia und Konstantinopel gegen Ende des vierten Jahrhunderts. Analyse der Quellen bei Johannes Chrysostomos*, OCA 187 (Rome 1970).

3. This civil conscription included the civil diocese of Thrace, in Europe, and the rest of the Eastern Empire except the Prefecture of Egypt (Augustalis).

4. On this story, see R. Taft, "The Authenticity of the Chrysostom Anaphora Revisited. Determining the Authorship of Liturgical Texts by Computer," OCP 56 (1990) 5–51.

5. See esp. his *Liturgie der ersten drei christlichen Jahrhunderte* (Tübingen 1870); *Sakramente und Sakramentalien in den drei ersten christlichen Jahrhunderte* (Tübingen 1872); *Liturgie des vierten Jahrhunderts und deren Reform* (Münster 1893).

6. *Vom geschichtlichen Werden der Liturgie* (Kempten and Munich 1923), and *Liturgie comparée* (Chevetogne 1934); English trans. *Comparative Liturgy* (Westminster, Md. 1958) from the 3rd French ed. (1953).

7. For example, Hellenic, Italic, Germanic, and Balto-Slavic.

8. For example, French, Italian, Spanish, Catalan, Portuguese, Romanian, Romansch, and Ladin within the Latin or Romance group; and German, Swedish, Danish, Norwegian, Icelandic, Dutch, English within the Teutonic or Germanic group.

9. For example, Siciliano, Calabrese, Napolitano, Romanesco, Romagnolo, Milanese, Veneto, and Ladino, to name but a few.

10. The evidence is provided by the *Protheoria* (PG 140:417–468), a liturgical commentary from Andida in Pamphylia ca. 1085–1095, that affirms explicitly its adherence to the rite of the Great Church (PG 140:429C).

11. A broad sampling can be found in Taft, "Mt. Athos."

3 The Byzantine Rite Becomes Imperial

Apart from its civil importance as the new capital and the preaching of Chrysostom, early Constantinople was known for little either culturally or ecclesiastically. It produced almost no literature of any importance, it was not a great intellectual or monastic center, and it was not the cradle of saints and martyrs. Furthermore, its homiletic and theological production was slim. The one exception was the notable interlude at the end of the fourth century during the episcopates of Gregory Nazianzen (379–381) and John Chrysostom (398–404)—but even their theology was Cappadocian or Antiochene and not Constantinopolitan. In none of these respects could Constantinople hold a candle to the great eastern ecclesiastical centers Alexandria and Antioch.[1] Yet its civil attributes—its sheer size, monumental architecture, and imperial court life—were legendary. Soon Constantinople would also become known for the splendors of its ritual, both imperial and ecclesiastical.

The Golden Age of Justinian and Beyond

By the sixth century, especially under the influence of Justinian I (527–565) who constructed the new Hagia Sophia, the Byzantine Rite became "imperial." Its eucharistic service in particular acquired greater ritual splendor and theological explicitation, especially as a result of the christological controversies. It accomplished this, in part, through the addition of new feasts, the creed (511), and several new chants such as the

28

Trisagion (ca. 438–439), the Monoġenes (535–536), and the Cheroubikon (573–574).[2] More significant for the development of the liturgy than these chants, however, were the processions they were meant to accompany. Indeed, except for an occasional reference to the dedication of a church[3] or to night vigils,[4] the sources in this epoch tell us almost nothing about Constantinopolitan liturgical services other than the eucharist and stational processions.

Inside Out: City as Church

I have already insisted on the singular unity in the Byzantine synthesis of the liturgy and its architectural/iconographic setting. But things were not always that way. The church as building, house of prayer, gathering place of the Christian assembly—*ho kyriakos oikos* rather than *he ekklesia*—became a significant reality in the rite of Constantinople only with the construction of Justinian's Hagia Sophia, dedicated on 27 December 537. Before that, Byzantine sources are remarkably reticent in attributing any symbolic significance to the church building.[5] As Cyril Mango points out in his anthology of Byzantine texts dealing with art and architecture:

> The "anagogical argument" (namely, that images serve to elevate our minds to immaterial realities), an argument derived from neo-Platonism, via the pseudo-Dionysian writings, does, in fact, appear from time to time, but it is the exception rather than the rule.[6]

There was little of symbolic or theological import attached to the Byzantine church building before Hagia Sophia. In fact, there was nothing distinctively "Byzantine" about pre-Justinianic churches in the capital. Most Byzantine liturgical description before Justinian—indeed, much of it in the entire period anterior to Iconoclasm (726–843)—simply ignored the church building. It dealt, rather, with what took place outside the church in the stational processions and services along the principal, porticoed streets (little more than alleys by modern standards) of Constantine's city.

From the new monumental center, southwest of the Acropolis and containing both the Constantinian Great Church (360) and the Imperial Palace, ran the city's four main arteries. Two of them ran along the coast of the peninsula, on the Golden Horn to the north and on the Propontis to the south. More important liturgically was the Mese, the traditional central cardo, which started as one at the Chalke Gate of the palace and ran past the Milion and through the Forum of Constantine to the Forum Tauri, where it divided. One branch headed southwest, threading the Fora Bovis and Arcadii and passing the Monastery of Stoudios (early fifth century) to exit the Theodosian Walls (413) at the Golden Gate and join the Via Egnatiana to Old Rome. The other arm branched north past the Holy Apostles Basilica to the Charisian Gate. Much of the liturgical activity that the Byzantines of the time thought important enough to record took place along these arteries and in their fora. This liturgical activity was fostered by the sheltering colonnades of these thoroughfares: the mid-fifth century *Notitia urbis* claims that there were fully fifty-two porticoes in the city.[8]

Disasters and heresies—both of which plagued the early Christian history of this city, if not in equal proportions then at least with equally portentous liturgical results—provided the main occasions for these outdoor services. Between 404 and 960 Constantinople was rocked by eighteen earthquakes.[9] Such earthquakes, as well as droughts or the fallout from volcanic eruptions, and man-made threats like the Avar siege of 626 or that of the Russes in 860,[10] would bring the populace into the streets to plead for salvation. And when granted, as it always was, the anniversary of this grace would be commemorated yearly in liturgical processions. Baldovin documents these occasions in detail, from the well-known myth of the heavenly origins of the Trisagion during the *lite* following the earthquake of 25 September 437 to the end of the millennium. He concludes, "Clearly, liturgical supplications and processions were the usual response to unusual danger in the liturgy of Constantinople, even well into the ninth century."[11]

Heresies were fewer, perhaps, but equally ominous. Arianism's multitudinous variants bled into the disputes over the Holy Spirit, and then gave way to Nestorianism and the far more subtle yet tenacious Monophysite christologies. Such theological disputes were the impetus behind many outdoor services in this emerging stational liturgy. Further, if less dramatic, occasions for such services were provided by church dedications, the transfer of relics,[12] and funerals (especially imperial). Later, with the developing calendar of memorials, one must include the cycle of synaxis celebrations in a determined church on set days.

The first evidence for this emerging stational liturgy appeared during the Arian ascendancy, when the beleaguered Gregory Nazianzen—Orthodox bishop of the capital from 379 to 381—attacked the pomp of church feasts and heaped scorn upon "the processions of the Greeks," which was an obvious reference to the Arians at that time.[13] The new emperor, Theodosius I (379-395), restored the churches to the Orthodox in 380, and by the time John Chrysostom took charge of the see in February 398, the Orthodox had regained the upper hand. But the Arian threat was not yet dissipated. According to Socrates (d. after 439), Chrysostom embarked on a vigorous policy of competitive stations to offset the still popular services of the Arians:

> The Arians . . . held their assemblies outside the city. So each week, whenever there was a feast—I mean Saturday and Sunday—on which it was customary to hold a synaxis in the churches, they congregated in public squares within the city gates and sang antiphonally odes composed in accord with the Arian belief. And this they did during the greater part of the night. In the morning, chanting the same antiphons, they processed through the center of the city and went outside the gates of the city to their place of assembly. . . . John [Chrysostom], concerned lest some of the more simple faithful be drawn away from the Church by such odes, set up some of his own people in opposition to them, so that they too, by devoting themselves to nocturnal hymnody, might obscure the effect of the Arians and confirm his own faithful in the profession of their own faith.[14]

Chrysostom's flock took up his initiative with gusto, bearing in procession silver crosses illumined with lighted tapers designed by the saint himself and paid for by the Empress Eudoxia (400–404). The torchlights of such processions along the coast turned the Propontis, according to Chrysostom, into a river of fire.[15]

Evidently the custom caught on, for Sozomen informs us that the processions continued even after the emperor put a stop to the Arian stations—thus, removing the original reason for the Orthodox counter-practice. Maybe the real reason why these popular outdoor services were maintained is to be found in Chrysostom's frequent complaints that Christian liturgy was not always the winner in its competition with the Hippodrome or circus for the people's attention.[16] Palladius refers to Chrysostom's nightly processions (*nychterinai litaneiai*), adding that some of the clergy, who preferred sleeping at night to watching and praying, were not enamored of their bishop's initiative.[17]

What began as a scrimmage with the Arians (and later the Monophysites) for control of the streets in the religious struggle for the soul of Byzantium,[18] thus perdured as a ploy in the less dramatic but longer-lasting competition with the blandishments of worldly entertainment for the attention of the urban populace of Late Antiquity. John of Ephesus (d. after 585) was a Monophysite Syriac church historian who was in Constantinople at the time of Justinian's predecessor (Justin I, 518–527). He describes in his *Church History* how the citizens and foreign visitors in the capital flocked to watch the entrance of the imperial retinue into church,[19] in the same way that crowds still gather in Rome for every appearance of the pope at some city church.

These Constantinopolitan stational services left an indelible stamp on the Divine Liturgy and other rites of the Great Church.[20] Entrances, processions, and accessions came to characterize all Byzantine liturgy. The enduring symbolism of these rites is demonstrated by their central place in the works of classic liturgical commentators, beginning with Maximus Confessor (ca. 630).[21] They could still be the subject of a brief treatise as late as Constantinopolitan Patriarch Gennadios II Scholarios, leader of the Orthodox at the Council of Florence in 1438-1439.[22]

Stational Impact on the Early Constantinopolitan Church

These outdoor processions had to end somewhere, and that somewhere was usually a church. The results were predictable. This processional activity was directly responsible for the characteristic shape of the early Constantinopolitan church, with numerous entrances on all four sides.[23] The major entrances were in the west facade,[24] which was preceded by an atrium or courtyard enclosed by a square portico. Processions would pause in the atrium—to await the completion of the introit courtesies of the hierarchs and dignitaries in the narthex, and the recitation of the Introit Prayer before the Royal Doors leading into the nave—before flooding into the nave with the dignitaries. Inside the church, the longitudinal axis between entrance and apse was emphasized, and the processions were guided to the sanctuary by floor markings[25] and the walled pathway of the solea, that funnelled the clergy and imperial entourage around the ambo and up to the gates of the templon or chancel that enclosed the sanctuary.

In this instance, *form follows function:* the liturgical arrangement of the Justinianic church building appears to have been dictated by the stational character of the urban rite. Its requirements were multiple:

1. a place for the people to gather while awaiting this solemn entrance, since—unlike in Old Rome—the people did not enter the church beforehand to welcome the arrival of the introit procession: hence the large west *atrium;*

2. an outbuilding, for the same reason, where the people could offer their gifts before the basilica was "opened liturgically" with the Introit Prayer and solemn entrance of the clergy and the imperial party: hence the emergence of the *skeuophylakion* rotunda, a separate building outside the church;[26]

3. since in the Constantinopolitan Introit (unlike the Introit of Old Rome) the clergy and people entered the church together, the need to provide easy and rapid access to the nave and

galleries from outside: hence, *the monumental doorways,* not only in the west facade but on all four sides of the church, and multiple *outside entrances* to the gallery stairwells;

4. a sheltered place for the patriarch and his escort, a) to await and greet the emperor before the Introit on days when the imperial party participated in the liturgy publicly; b) to await the arrival of the stational procession on days when the dignitaries did not take part in the stations; c) to say the Introit Prayer before the Royal Doors or principal west entrance into the nave; and d) at other services, to perform the rites that preceded the patriarch's solemn entrance into the church: hence the monumental *narthex.*[27]

A further peculiarity of the Constantinopolitan arrangement was the elevated synthronon and cathedra in the apse. This came about not because of the stations, but so that the bishop could be seen while preaching from the throne: another fundamental element in the liturgy of this period.[28] Other characteristics—such as the chancel and ambo, and the enclosed solea walkway connecting them[29]—are not peculiar to Byzantium and are found, *mutatis mutandis,* in Late Antique church arrangements in Rome, Syria, and Mesopotamia. The galleries and their use remain a separate problem, but they, too, are found elsewhere and cannot be considered proper only to Constantinople and its liturgy.[30] What was peculiar to Constantinople in these arrangements was required by the urban cathedral rite: the liturgical disposition of the pre-Studite Constantinopolitan monastic church remains to be discovered.

The Importance of the Entrances

Lest one think I am attributing too much importance to the processional Introit, let the sources themselves speak of the lengths to which the Byzantines would go to formalize and stylize this major feature of church life in old Constantinople. For this, one must turn to imperial ceremonial. By the time of Justinian, Constantinopolitan imperial corteges were so impressive that they had become a topos for regal splendor. Leontius the presbyter, a popular preacher in the capital around

552–565, used them regularly as a homiletic foil to the humility of the Heavenly King.[31] It is little wonder that the participation of the emperor gave a special "imperial" tone to liturgical services.

The imperial ritual, both ecclesiastical and secular, is described in fragmentary fashion by numerous sources. Especially important are the *ex professo* ceremonial books of the imperial court, such as the *De cerimoniis aulae Byzantinae* or *Book of Ceremonies* compiled from earlier sources by Emperor Constantine VII Porphyrogenitus (913–920, 945–959),[32] and the mid-fourteenth century *De officiis* or *Office Book* of Pseudo-Codinus.[33] The emperor's progress to the church for the liturgy as detailed in the *Book of Ceremonies* was a stational procession in microcosm, in which the cortege moved from designated spot to designated spot, with a set ritual order for each stop along the route. The force with which this struck the onlooker is obvious from the description of Harun ibn-Yahya, an Arab prisoner held hostage at the court of Basil I (867–886) in the last quarter of the ninth century. His fantastic description of the imperial progress from palace to church, with an entourage of over 55,000 imperial officials, illustrates the impact of this solemn accession.[34] Things seemed to have changed little in the succeeding centuries if we are to believe the Russian pilgrim Ignatius of Smolensk who was present at the crowning of Manuel II Paleologus (third from the last of the Byzantine emperors, 1391–1425) in Hagia Sophia on 11 February 1392. According to Ignatius' equally exaggerated account, "The imperial procession was very slow-paced, so that three hours [were consumed going] from the main doors to the chamber."[35]

Outside In: Church Building as Cosmos

In fact, things had changed and changed considerably. From the time of Justinian I, Byzantine liturgical description and commentary became more and more concerned with what took place inside the church, with the church itself, and with its symbolic meaning. The Justinianic era introduced changes not only in church arrangement but also in perception. Previously, commentators on churches in the capital remarked on their great beauty, and waxed eloquently on what would eventually become a topos: the startling effect created by the light flooding in from the windows. They even referred to the domed roof as the heavens.[36] With Hagia Sophia and its liturgy, the perspective changed. In no liturgical tradition has one edifice played so seminal a role as Justinian's Hagia Sophia. Both the shape of the Byzantine Rite and the vision of its meaning—enacted on a smaller scale in later buildings—were determined in this cathedral church. What was most new about this building, far more than its startling architecture, was the *vision* created by its marvellous interior. This vision was to have a formative influence on the spirit of the ritual Hagia Sophia was built to house.

A Christian church is not a temple. Originally the community, and not some material shrine, was the dwelling of God's presence.[37] In time it became customary to see the church building as a symbol of the mysteries it housed. Not until Justinian, however, did Constantinople have a vessel worthy to reflect this reality. With Hagia Sophia the *domus ecclesiae* became the New Temple and Justinian surpassed Solomon, as the legend has him exclaim on the occasion of its dedication in 537.[38]

The Byzantines did not invent the notion of the church as a Platonic image of the cosmos, reaching from God's throne upon the Cherubim to the lower realm where human life is enacted.[39] Hagia Sophia, however, gave a completely new expression to this concept. The awesome splendors of its vastness and the sparkling brilliance of its light led observers to exclaim with remarkable consistency that here, indeed, was heaven on earth, the heavenly sanctuary, a second firmament, image of the cosmos, and throne of the very glory of God.[40] As with all great buildings, the structure itself—not its decoration—created this impression. The original decoration of Hagia Sophia was minimal.[41] Only later would much smaller structures of a poorer age require the explicitation of this symbolism representatively, in mosaic and fresco, in accord with the more literal spirit of the post-iconoclastic age.

Long before such explication in mosaic and fresco, the cosmic symbolism was embedded in the liturgical texts of the epoch. Let us return to the Introit. The procession has arrived, the liturgy is about to begin. The patriarch is in the narthex, where he has greeted the emperor; both are awaiting the signal to enter the church. From their chamber beneath the great ambo, the psalmists intone the *Ho Monogenes* troparion,[42] traditional refrain of the Introit Psalm (LXX Ps 94:1-6a).

At this signal, the patriarch goes before the Royal Doors to say the Introit Prayer: the opening collect of the Divine Liturgy in the two traditional Constantinopolitan formularies of St. Basil and St. Chrysostom. To the patriarch—his gaze into the nave framed by the open doors and interior western buttresses, his view encompassing the central axis of ambo, solea, and sanctuary, brilliantly bathed in the rays of the sun as it streamed through the windows in the conch of the apse[43]—the words of the prayer must certainly have seemed fulfilled, evoking the vision of the heavenly sanctuary resplendent to the East, as if before his very eyes:

> O Lord and Master, our God, who in heaven has established the orders and armies of angels and archangels to minister unto your majesty, grant that the holy angels may enter with us, and with us serve and glorify your goodness . . .[44]

This typology—in which the earthly church is seen to image the heavenly sanctuary where the God of heaven dwells, and the earthly liturgy is a "concelebration" in the worship which the Heavenly Lamb and the angelic choirs offer before the throne of God—was the first level of Byzantine liturgical interpretation, reflected in such fifth-sixth century liturgical additions as this Introit Prayer and the Cheroubikon (A.D. 573-74).[45] Such liturgical interpretation was systematized in the *Mystagogy* of Maximus Confessor ca. 630.[46]

On the eve of Iconoclasm, therefore, a certain synthesis of liturgy and mystagogy had already emerged. In the next period this system would undergo developments radical enough to be called changes, but in sufficient continuity with what preceded to be deemed evolution, not revolution.

Notes

1. Beck, "Constantinople" (previous chap., note 1) esp. 31-35.

2. See my entries under these titles in ODB; for the Creed and Cheroubikon, see Taft, *Great Entrance* chs. 2 and 11. The Trisagion first appeared in Constantinopolitan processional rogations in 438-439, but became a permanent element of the eucharistic liturgy only at the beginning of the 6th century.

3. John Malalas (ca. 490-570's), contemporary of Justinian, *Chronographia* 18, ed. L. Dindorf, *Ioannis Malalae Chronographia,* CSHB (Bonn 1831) 495.9-16 = PG 97:716; Theophanes Confessor (ca. 760-817), *Chronographia* 18, ed. C. de Boor, *Theophanis Chronographia,* 2 vols. (Leipzig 1883-1885) I, 238.18-24 = PG 108:520; cf. Taft, *Great Entrance* 110 (where I identify Malalas with John III Scholasticus, patriarch of Constantinople from 565-577, an identification now rejected by Byzantine historians; see B. Baldwin, "Malalas, John," in ODB 2:1275).

4. As in Justinian's ruling of 528 ordering all the clergy in each church to chant nocturns (*nykterina*) daily, and not just matins and vespers; Justinian, *Code* I, iii, 42:24 (10), P. Krüger, *Corpus iuris civilis,* vol. 2 (Berlin 1900) 28; cf. Taft, *Hours* 186 and ch. 9 passim.

5. This is borne out by a perusal of the relevant Byzantine texts in Mango, *Art.*

6. Ibid., xiv.

7. On this concept and its development in Late Antiquity, the basic study is Baldovin.

8. Ibid., 171.

9. Ibid., 171.

10. Ibid., 189.

11. Ibid., 186-189.

12. For an early instance, see the procession described in the *Vita* of St. Marcian, in R. Taft, "Byzantine Liturgical Evidence in the *Life of St. Marcian the Oeconomos:* Concelebration and the Preanaphoral Rites," OCP 48 (1982) 159-170.

13. *Oratio* 38, 5-6, PG 36:316; Baldovin 181.

14. Socrates, *Church History* VI, 8 = PG 67:688-9. Cf. Sozomen (ca. 439-450), *Church History* VIII, 8, ed. J. Bidez, GCS 50 (Berlin 1960) 360-361 = PG 67:1536.

15. E.g. *Hom. dicta postquam reliquiae martyrum* . . . 2, CPG 4441.1 = PG 63:470, describing a transfer of martyr's relics to the suburb of Drypia on the Via Egnatia, 13.5 km west of the city, towards the end of his first year in Constantinople: Baldovin 183. Cf. Chrysostom, *De S. Hieromartyre Phoca*, PG 50:699, which Baldovin (183) cites.

16. *Hom. dicta postquam reliquiae martyrum* . . . 1, PG 63:461; *Hom. adv. eos qui non adfuerant* 1, CPG 4441.4 = PG 63:477; *Hom. in illud: 'Pater meus usque modo operatur'* 1, CPG 4441.10 = PG 63:511.

17. Palladios, *Dialogue on the Life of St. John Chrysostom* V, 147-150 = Palladios, *Dialogue sur la vie de Jean Chrysostome* I, ed. A.-M. Malingrey, P. Leclercq, Sources chrétiennes 341 (Paris 1988) 124.

18. Baldovin 184-186. As Baldovin (186) points out, the attempt of Emperor Anastasius to gain control of the processions ca. 496, as reported by Theodore Lector, underscored their political and civil importance: Theodoros Anagnostes, *Kirchengeschichte*, ed. G. C. Hansen, GCS 54, 2nd ed. (Berlin 1971) no. 468, p. 134.

19. *Church History* III.3, Iohannis Ephesini, *Historiae ecclesiasticae pars tertia*, ed. F. W. Brooks, Corpus scriptorum Christianorum orientalium 105-106: Scriptores Syri 54-55 (Paris/Louvain 1935-1936) text 138, versio 102.

20. See Mateos, *Célébration;* Taft, *Beyond East and West* ch. 11; Mathews chs. 4-7; Baldovin ch. 6.

21. See Taft, ''Liturgy.''

22. *Peri ton hieron eisodon* (''On the Sacred Entrances''), in L. Petit, X. A. Siderides, M. Jugie (eds.), *Oeuvres complètes de Gennade Scholarius*, Tome III: *Oeuvres polémiques, questions théologiques, écrits apologétiques* (Paris 1930) 196-99.

23. Hagia Sophia, for example, has fifty-six doors on the ground floor: nineteen of them leading into the nave and six of them at the main processional entrance area in the narthex. On all questions of church planning in the early churches of Constantinople, see Mathews.

24. See the work of Strube, cited below in note 30.

25. On floor markings and their ceremonial use, see G. P. Majeska, ''Notes on the Archeology of St. Sophia of Constantinople: The Green Marble Bands on the Floor,'' DOP 32 (1978) 299-308; P. Schreiner, ''Omphalion und Rota Porphyretica. Zum Kaiserzeremoniell in Konstantinopel und Rom,'' in S. Dufrenne (ed.), *Byzance et les Slaves. Mélanges Ivan Dujčev* (Paris 1979) 401-410. They are mentioned in 1200 by the Russian pilgrim Anthony of Novgorod, Xr. M. Loparev (ed.), *Kniga palomchik. Skazanie mest svjatyx vo Tsaregrade Antonija Novgorodskago v 1200 godu*, Pravoslavnyj Palestiniskij Sbornik, vypusk 51, vol. 17.3 (St. Petersburg 1899) 78, 81; French trans. in Mme. B. de Khitrowo, *Itinéraires russes en Orient* (Geneva 1889) 95, 99.

26. See Mathews, esp. 155–162, 178. George P. Majeska of the University of Maryland is working on a new study on the skeuophylakion, incorporating the latest archaeological and literary findings. I am grateful to Professor Majeska for providing me with a copy of the initial draft of this excellent study.

27. The perdurance of the narthex and, in some cases, the esonarthex (in the Justinianic period—surely not afterward), cannot be ascribed to the catechumenate, which was largely nonexistent probably during the 6th, certainly by the 7th century.

28. See my article "Sermon" in ODB 3:1880–81.

29. This enclosed walkway served to keep the sanctuary area free for liturgical use and to facilitate the comings and goings of the lectors and others from the sanctuary to the ambo.

30. I discuss this question in my review of Ch. Strube, *Die westliche Eingangsseite der Kirchen von Konstantinopel in justinianischer Zeit*, OCP 42 (1976) 296–303. See also, T. F. Mathews' review in *Byzantinische Zeitschrift* 70 (1977) 385.

31. *Hom.* 2.141–162; 3/3a.18–29, 61–96; 12.127–142, C. Datema, P. Allen (eds.), *Leontii Presbyteri Constantinopolitani Homiliae*, Corpus Christianorum, series Graeca 17 (Turnhout 1987) 90–91, 150–153, 156–159, 385–386; English trans. by the same authors, Leontius Presbyter of Constantinople, *Fourteen Homilies*, Byzantina Australiensia 9 (Brisbane 1991) 44, 51–53, 175.

32. Vogt, texte I-II.

33. Ps.-Kodinos, *Traité des offices*, ed. J. Verpeaux (Paris 1966).

34. A. A. Vasiliev, "Harun-ibn-Yahya and his Description of Constantinople," *Seminarium Kondakovianum* 5 (1932) 158–159. These awesome imperial entrances have been studied at length by D. Th. Beljaev, "Ezhednevnye priemy vizantijskix tsarej i prazdnichnye vyxody ix v xram Sv. Sofii v IX–XI vv.," *Zapiski Imperatorskago Russkago arxeologicheskago obshchestva*, n.s. 6 (1893) i–xlvii, 1–309; esp. chs. 4–5; id., "Bogomol'nye vyxody vizantijskix tsarej v gorodskie i prigorodnye xramy Konstantinopolja," *Zapiski klassicheskago otdelenija Imperatorskago Russkago arxeologicheskago obshchestva* 4 (1906) 1–189.

35. G. P. Majeska, *Russian Travelers to Constantinople in the Fourteenth and Fifteenth Centuries*, Dumbarton Oaks Studies 19 (Washington 1984), text 106–107; commentary 423–424. The "chamber" (*chertog*) was the *metatorion* or imperial loge in the nave of Hagia Sophia where the emperor attended services; cf. Mathews 96, 133–134; Vogt, commentaire I, 61; J.-P. Papadopoulos, "Le mutatorium des églises byzantines," in *Mémorial L. Petit*, Archives de l'Orient chrétien 1 (Bucharest 1948) 366–372.

36. For example, Gregory Nazianzen, *Or. 18*, 39, PG 35:1037; Mango, *Art* 26.

37. Mk 14:58; Jn 2:21; 1 Cor 3:16, 6:19; 2 Cor 6:16; 1 Pet 2:5; Eph 2:19-22; cf. Y. M.-J. Congar, *The Mystery of the Temple* (Westminster, Md. 1962) ch. 8.

38. See the 8–9th c. account in *Anonymi Narratio de aedificatione templi S. Sophiae* 27, ed. Th. Preger, *Scriptores originum Constantinopolitanarum*, BSGRT (Leipzig 1901, reprint 1989) 105.

39. Though first systematized for Byzantium ca. 630 by Maximus Confessor (d. 660) in his *Mystagogy* (1–5, PG 91:664–84 = Maximus Confessor, *Selected Writings*, The Classics of Western Spirituality [N.Y./Mahwah, N.J./Toronto 1985] 186-195), the notion of temple as microcosm is a commonplace of human religiosity. Cf. M. Eliade, *Images and Symbols. Studies in Religious Symbolism* (N.Y. 1969) ch. 1; idem, *The Myth of the Eternal Return* (London 1955) ch. 1; idem, *The Sacred and the Profane* (N.Y. 1959) ch. 1. It is apparently first applied to the Christian church building in a 6th c. poem on the cathedral of Edessa: H. Goussen (ed.), "Über eine 'Sugitha' auf die Kathedrale von Edessa," *Le Muséon* 38 (1925) 117-36 (trans. Mango, *Art* 57-60); cf. A. Grabar, "Le témoignage d'une hymne syriaque sur l'architecture de la cathédrale d'Edesse au VIe siècle et sur la symbolique de l'édifice chrétien," CA 2 (1948) 41-67.

40. E.g., Procopius, *De aedificiis* I, i.61, ed. H. B. Dewing and G. Downey, *Procopius* VII, Loeb Classical Library (Cambridge, Mass. 1954) 26 = Mango, *Art* 76; Adammanus (ca. 705), *De locis sanctis libri tres.* Itinera Hierosolymitana saec. III–VIII, Corpus scriptorum ecclesiasticorum Latinorum 38:28; Germanus I (ca. 730), *Historia ecclesiastica* 1 and 4, P. Meyendorff, *Germanus* 56–59; Michael Psellus (11th c.), *Oratio 35*, Michael Psellus, *Oratoria minora*, ed. A. R. Littlewood, BSGRT (Leipzig 1985) 131–132 = PG 122:912; Nicetas Choniata (1206), *Historia* 4, ed. I. Bekker, CSHB (Bonn 1835) 782.

41. Its present decorative program dates from ca. 866–913, after the defeat of Iconoclasm: Mango, *Materials* 93-4.

42. See my article "Monogenes, Ho" in ODB 2:1397.

43. There is a photograph of this exact view in Kähler, illustr. 23; cf. the description, ibid. 28ff.

44. LEW 312.15-30 (left col.). This is the original Constantinopolitan Introit Prayer. The text, given loc. cit. (right col.) with the Chrysostom Liturgy, is an Italo-Greek peculiarity unknown in the Constantinopolitan redactions of the euchology: Jacob, "Tradition," 109-38; cf. Taft, *Great Entrance* xxxi-ii, 128-9.

45. On this chant, see Taft, *Great Entrance* 53-118.

46. See note 39 above.

4 The Dark Ages and Iconoclasm

The seventh century was for the East what the fifth had been for the West: the end of the Roman Empire. The ancient classical world died a turbulent death as Slavic tribes crossed the Danube around 580 and settled in the Balkans and Greece, and the armies of Islam severed Syria, Palestine, Egypt, and North Africa from the once-Roman and Christian world forever.

Nature and humanity share responsibility for the debacle.[1] Plague, drought, and continuous earthquakes depopulated the cities. Constantinople alone is said to have lost 300,000 inhabitants in the bubonic plague of 542. Justinian's costly attempts to reconquer the western territories, previously lost to the Germanic tribes, brought an exhausted empire to the brink of economic collapse, leaving it open to Persian advances in the East. After Heraclius' (610–641) recovery of the eastern provinces and Jerusalem, a greater and more permanent menace swept out of Arabia. Within fifteen years of Heraclius' definitive victory over the Persians in 626–627, Syria, Palestine, and Egypt were lost again—this time forever. Thereafter, the empire was threatened continuously on every flank, from the Arab sieges of Constantinople (674–678 and 717–718), and the ninth-century incursions from the north by the still unconverted Bulgars— they accepted Byzantine Christianity only in 864–865—to the fatal Turkish threat to the east.

One by one, the great centers of Alexandria, Antioch, and Jerusalem were lost to Islam, while the Monophysite movement mortally weakened the Orthodox Church in those patriarchates. The Patristic Age and Greek dominance of the East were brought to a close with the empire sinking into feudalism, as once great metropolises shriveled into beleaguered provincial fortresses.

By the time the Council in Trullo met at Constantinople in 691–692, the Byzantine Church had turned inward, consolidating its own forces while turning its face against the usages of other traditions, especially the Latin West. But the worst was yet to come, as the Orthodox Church faced the most serious internal crisis of its history—Iconoclasm (726–843). This was followed by an equally grave external challenge, the growing estrangement from Rome over jurisdiction in Bulgaria. The latter led to the first serious break in the so-called "Photian Schism" of 867. Cyril Mango calls this period—from the advent of Heraclius in 610 until about the middle of the ninth century—the Byzantine "Dark Centuries."[2]

What do we know of the liturgy during this period of decline? For the liturgical rites themselves, this was, above all, a period of continuity. The Rite of the Great Church continued to be celebrated, even if in more straightened circumstances. But it was also a period of consolidation and retrenchment enforced by the reduction in scale of public life and its monuments, and a period of realignment in response to Iconoclasm.

Continuity

By the time of Justinian and his immediate successors, at the height of what I have called the "imperial phase" of Byzantine liturgical history, the Rite of the Great Church can be said to have reached its apogee. This Constantinopolitan cathedral rite continued in use throughout the following centuries as it was reinterpreted, even superceded, by later developments. As late as the fifteenth century, Symeon of Thessalonika testified to its continued use in that metropolis under his episcopate (1416/17–1429), but noted that in Constantinople itself, the rite did not outlast the Latin occupation of 1204–1261.[3]

One may ask, however, whether the perdurance of this rite in Hagia Sophia and the other churches of the capital in the post-Justinianic period was similar to the survival in court life of much that is found in the tenth-century *Book of Ceremonies*.

As more than one Byzantinist has pointed out, this document, like many canonical collections, is a compilation of diverse levels of material. Some of its rituals are descriptions of actual celebrations.[4] The continual updating of its prescriptions under Constantine VII's successors Romanus II (959–963) and Nicephorus Phocas (963–969) indicate its ongoing relevance to actual usage.[5] But not all of them can be taken uncritically as an actual mirror of tenth-century Byzantine society. By this time the government had retreated somewhat from the public scene. Indeed, in his Preface to the *De cerimoniis*, Constantine VII explicitly states his aim to restore traditions that had already decayed.[6] For Cyril Mango, then, "the Book of Ceremonies is essentially an antiquarian work rather than a practical manual."[7] This is not surprising. The stylized formality of Byzantine public life, with its predilection for *taxis* or order,[8] necessitated a heavy dose of ritual conservatism in court and church. Thus, numerous aspects of court life that the *Book of Ceremonies* described as still current—the Hippodrome, chariot racing, the Factions, luxurious public bathing, reclining at table—may no longer have been in general social use:

> These survivals suggest that the evocation of an extinct life-style, that of the Empire in its greatness, was a deliberate component of court ceremonial. Which is why, perhaps, the *Book of Ceremonies* is what it is—not a guide to existing procedure, but a collection of ancient precedents.[9]

Can something analogous be said of the survival of the Rite of the Great Church after the "Dark Ages"? During the seventh and eighth centuries, when the empire was battered by two hundred years of ceaseless warfare on its outer flanks, the liturgy doubtlessly continued to be celebrated in Hagia Sophia and the other sanctuaries of the capital with its stational processions and whatever else could be mustered of its former imperial splendor. A variety of Constantinopolitan sources witness to this liturgical continuity right up until the Fourth Crusade (1204). These include: the tenth-century Typikon of the Great Church[10]; the earliest extant liturgical ordo of the stations in codex *Paris Coislin 213*, a euchology ms dating from 1027 AD[11]; the Patriarchal Euchology of the eleventh-twelfth

century codex *Grottaferrata Gb I¹²*; and the eleventh-century
Pontifical Diataxis of the twelfth-century codex *British Library
Add. 34060*, reporting the patriarchal liturgy from the same
period.[13] Yet one can legitimately ask whether some of the liturgical prescriptions in these sources should not be subjected to
the same hermeneutic as those preserved in the *Book of Ceremonies*. Similar to the antiquarian relics of the Italian Renaissance
that existed in papal court life until Pope Paul VI cleaned house,
some of the liturgical prescriptions concerning the Byzantine
Rite—even though they were still celebrated at Hagia Sophia
and a handful of other places—might simply be remnants of
a by-gone era, the former splendors of an empire in decline.[14]

Consolidation

Liturgical sources show that by the ninth century the Great
Church of Constantinople had evolved its complete cathedral
liturgical system, codified in the still extant tenth-century
Typikon of the Great Church.[15] Its components included a native calendar[16] and its accompanying lectionary system,[17] its
own eucharistic liturgy[18] and other sacramental rites,[19] as well
as a cathedral liturgy of the hours, the *Asmatike Akolouthia* or
"Sung Office" of the Great Church.[20] Its evolution was especially marked by the development of a system of stational services. But in the organization of their liturgical life, apart from
the liturgy of the eucharist the monasteries of the patriarchate
were still marching to the beat of their own, different drum.
The monks of the capital, called *akoimetoi* or "sleepless" because they celebrated in shifts an uninterrupted cursus of
hours, had their distinct office.[21]

Change: The New Mystagogy

Significant changes in liturgical understanding and practice
soon rent the fabric of this "imperial" liturgical system. Even
before the liturgical reforms consequent upon the victory over
Iconoclasm,[22] the evolution of Byzantine liturgical interpretation in the century from Maximus (ca. 630) to Germanus I (ca.
730) betrays this clearly. By the eighth century, on the eve of
the iconoclastic crisis, the traditional Maximiam "cosmic" litur-

gical interpretation began to give way before a more literal and representational narrative vision of the liturgical *historia*. While not abandoning the cosmic, heavenly-liturgy typology—biblically warranted in the Epistle to the Hebrews and the Apocalypse, and inherited from Maximus' *Mystagogy*—Germanus integrated another level of interpretation into Byzantine liturgical understanding; one that was equally rooted in the New Testament and also found, though far less prominently, in Maximus and other earlier Byzantine liturgical writings. This was the interpretation of the eucharist, not only as the anamnesis of, but also as actual figure of salvation history in Jesus.

In an earlier study I traced the hagiopolite provenance of this Antiochene-style *historia* to Germanus via Theodore of Mopsuestia (d. 428).[23] Writing at the end of the fourth century—most probably at Antioch in the decade before becoming bishop of Mopsuestia in 392—Theodore was the first to synthesize the two themes of the historical self-offering of Jesus and the liturgy of the heavenly Christ in his *Catechetical Homilies* (15–16). Theodore offers a synthesis of ritual representation in which the Jesus-anamnesis is conceived as a dramatic reenactment of the paschal mystery encompassing the whole eucharistic rite: the earthly celebrant is seen as an image of the heavenly high priest, and the earthly liturgy as an icon of his eternal heavenly oblation. With Germanus, these two leitmotifs become an integral part of the Byzantine synthesis.

How Germanus achieved this synthesis can be seen in his interpretation of the two entrances. The Lesser Introit, or "Little Entrance" (*He mikra eisodos*), is interpreted in purely cosmic terms in its accompanying Introit Prayer—a traditional text found in all Byzantine euchology manuscripts and surely known to Germanus.[24] He abandons this traditional symbolism, however, preferring a salvation-history interpretation of the entrance as imaging forth the coming of Christ into the world:

> The entrance of the Gospel shows the appearance of the Son
> of God into this world, as the apostle says, "When he—i.e.,

God the Father—brings the first-born into the world, He says: Let all His angels worship Him" (Heb 1:6).[25]

Elsewhere, Germanus simply juxtaposes the two interpretative strata. He does this, for example, in his explanation of the Major Introit or "Great Entrance" (*He megale eisodos*), interpreted in the liturgical text by its accompanying Cheroubikon chant that was introduced into the liturgy under Justin II in 573–574:

> We who mystically represent the Cherubim and sing the thrice-holy hymn to the life-giving Trinity, let us now lay aside all worldly care to receive the King of All escorted unseen by the angelic corps! Alleluia!

Germanus does not abandon the hermeneutic of the liturgical text:

> By means of the procession of the deacons, and the representation (*historia*) of the ripidia bearing an image of the Seraphim, the Cherubic Hymn shows the entrance of the saints and all the just, entering together before the cherubic powers and angelic hosts, invisibly going before Christ the Great King proceeding to the Mystical Sacrifice . . . (37).

He enriches the text, however, with the new historicism:

> It is also in imitation of the burial of Christ, just as Joseph took down the body from the cross and wrapped it in a clean shroud, and after anointing it with spices and myrrh, carried it with Nicodemus and buried it in a new monument cut from rock. The altar and depository is the antitype of the Holy Sepulchre, that is, the holy table on which is placed the immaculate and all-holy body (37).

This encroachment of a more literal tradition upon an earlier, mystical level of Byzantine interpretation, coincided with the beginnings of the struggle against Iconoclasm (726–843). This was the time when shifts in Byzantine piety led to such growth in the cult of images that Orthodoxy found itself locked in mortal combat, defending this new expression of radical incarnational-realism against the conservative reaction that promoted a more symbolic and, ultimately, iconoclastic spiritualism. Symbolism and portrayal are not the same thing either in art or in liturgy.[26] The effect of the new, more literal mentality was immediately detectable in three different ways: [1] in the representational mystagogy integrated into the earlier Maximian tradition by Germanus ca. 730; [2] in the condemnation, by the Seventh Ecumenical Council in 787, of the teaching of the iconoclastic council of 754 that the eucharist is the only valid symbol of Christ;[27] [3] and, ultimately—as I hope to show in chapter 6—in the iconographic program of the Middle-Byzantine church.

Notes

1. See Mango, *Architecture* 161.
2. Loc. cit.
3. PG 155:553D, 625B.
4. M. McCormick, *Eternal Victory. Triumphal Rulership in Late Antiquity, Byzantium, and the Early Medieval West* (Cambridge/Paris 1986) 160.
5. Ibid. 175–176; J. B. Bury, "The Ceremonial Book of Constantine Porphyrogennetos," *English Historical Review* 22 (1907) 217–221.
6. Vogt, texte I, 1–2; cf. McCormick (note 4 above) 175–176.
7. Mango, "Daily Life," 346; also, Averil Cameron, "The Construction of Court Ritual: The Byzantine *Book of Ceremonies,* in D. Cannadine, S. Price, *Rituals of Royalty. Power and Ceremonial in Traditional Societies* (Cambridge 1987), 106–36.
8. Cf. A. Kazhdan, G. Constable, *People and Power in Byzantium. An Introduction to Modern Byzantine Studies* (Washington 1982) 60–66, 126, 134, 137, 158, 161.
9. Mango, "Daily Life," 352.
10. Mateos, *Typicon* I–II.
11. Dmitrievskij II, 1009–1111, fully exploited in Baldovin 202–204. This ms has been the object of two doctoral dissertations under the direction of M. Arranz at the Pontifical Oriental Institute, Rome: the first part of the codex (ff. 1–100) is critically edited by J. Duncan, *Coislin 213. Euchologe de la Grande Église* (Rome 1983); the rest (ff. 101–211), though still unpublished, is edited by J. M. Maj, *Coislin 213. Eucologio della Grande Chiesa. Manoscritto della Biblioteca Nazionale di Parigi. Testo critico annotato dei ff. 101–211* (Rome 1990).
12. Cf. Arranz, "Hesperinos," 112, 115–116.
13. R. Taft, "The Pontifical Liturgy of the Great Church according to a Twelfth-Century Diataxis in Codex *British Museum Add. 34060,*" I: OCP 45 (1979) 279–307; II: OCP 46 (1980) 89–124.

14. As I have already noted above, the historico-social "contextualizing" of liturgical documents is an obvious necessity that the historians of eastern liturgy—few and still occupied with the preliminaries in an embryonic discipline—have not yet attended to adequately; cf. R. Taft, "Response to the Berakah Award: Anamnesis," *Worship* 59 (1985) 314–15.

15. Mateos, *Typicon* I-II.

16. Ibid.; H. Delehaye, *Synaxarium Ecclesiae Constantinopolitanae*, Propylaeum ad Acta Sanctorum Novembris, *Acta Sanctorum* XI (Brussels 1902); A. Ehrhard, *Überlieferung und Bestand der hagiographischen und homiletischen Literatur im byzantinischen Reich*, I-III.1, TU 50–52.1 (Leipzig 1936–1943), III.2, TU 52.2 (Berlin 1952) esp. I, 28–33; S. A. Morcelli, *Menologion ton Euangelion Heortastikon sive Kalendarium Ecclesiae Constantinopolitanae* (Rome 1788).

17. On the development of the lectionary, in addition to the works cited in the previous note, see, inter alia, especially the numerous studies of Yvonne Burns, *The Byzantine Weekday Gospel Lectionaries*, New Testament Tools and Studies (Leiden, forthcoming); "Chapter Numbers in Greek and Slavonic Gospel Codices," *New Testament Studies* 23.3 (Cambridge 1977); " 'The Canaanites' and other Additional Lections in Early Slavonic Lectionaries," *Revue des études sudest européennes* 12 (Bucharest 1975); "The Greek Manuscripts Connected by their Lection System with the Palestinian Syriac Gospel Lectionaries," *Studia Biblica* 2, Journal for the Study of the New Testament Supplement, series 2 (Sheffield 1980) 13–28; "The Historical Events that Occasioned the Inception of the Byzantine Gospel Lectionaries," JöB 32.4 (1982) 119–127; "The Lectionary of the Patriarch of Constantinople," *Studia Patristica* 15.1, TU 128 (Berlin 1984) 515–520; "A Newly Discovered Family 13 Manuscript and the Ferrar Lection System," *Studia Patristica* 17.1 (Oxford 1982) 278–289; "The Numbering of the Johannine Saturdays and Sundays in Early Greek and Slavonic Gospel Lectionaries," *Palaeobulgarica* 1.2 (Sofia 1977) 43–55; "The Weekday Lection System of Miroslav's Gospel," *Narodnog Muzeja u Beogradu* 6 (1970) 259–286. Also, K. Aland, *Kurzgefaßte Liste der griechischen Handschriften des Neuen Testaments*, ANTF 1 (Berlin 1963); id., "Die griechischen Handschriften des Neuen Testaments. Ergänzungen zur *Kurzgefaßten Liste*," Fortsetzungsliste VII, in *Materialen zur neutestamentlichen Handschriftenkunde* 1, ANTF 3 (Berlin 1969), with additions in J. Noret, "Manuscrits grecs du Nouveau Testament," Lectionnaires, *Analecta Bollandiana* 87 (1969) 464–8; A. Baumstark, *Nicht evangelische syrische Perikopenordnungen des ersten Jahrtausends*, Liturgiegeschichtliche Forschungen 15 (Münster 1921); J. N. Birdsall, "Two Lectionaries in Birmingham," JTS 35 (1984) 448–454; W. C. Braithwaite, "The Lection System of the Codex Macedonianus," JTS 5 (1904) 265–274; Mary-Lyon Dolezal, "The Lectionary and Textual Criticism," *Abstracts*

of Papers, Fourteenth Annual Byzantine Studies Conference, The Menil Collection and the University of St. Thomas (Houston 1988) 31–32; N. Dragomir, "Studiu istorico-liturgic privind textele biblice din cărțile de cult ale Bisericii Ortodoxe," *Studii teologice* 33 (1981) 207–268; P. H. Droosten, "Proems of Liturgical Lections and Gospels," JTS 6 (1901) 99–106; H. Engberding, "Das Rätsel einer Reihe vom 16. Sonntagsepisteln," OC 52 (1968) 81–86; G. Garitte, "Analyse d'un lectionnarire byzantino-géorgien des Évangiles (Sin. géorg. 84), *Le Muséon* 91 (1978) 105–152; C. R. Gregory, *Textkritik des Neuen Testaments*, 3 vols. (Leipzig 1900, 1902, 1909); P.-M. Gy, "La question du système des lectures de la liturgie byzantine," *Miscellanea liturgica in onore di S.E.G. Lercaro* (Rome 1967) II, 251–261; K. Junak, "Zu den griechischen Lektionaren und ihrer Überlieferung der Katholischen Briefe," in K. Aland (ed.), *Die alten Übersetzungen des Neuen Testaments, die Kirchenväterzitate und Lektionare*, ANTF 5 (Berlin/N.Y. 1972) 498–591; B. Metzger, "Greek Lectionaries and a Critical Edition of the Greek New Testament," ibid. 479–497; id., "A Comparison of the Palestinian Syriac Lectionary and the Greek Gospel Lectionary," in E. E. Ellis, M. Wilcox (eds.), *Neotestamentica et Semitica. Studies in Honour of Matthew Black* (Edinburgh 1969) 209–220; A. Kniazeff, "La lecture de l'Ancien et du Nouveau Testament dans le rite byzantin," in Mons. Cassien, B. Botte (eds.), *La prière des heures*, Lex orandi 35 (Paris 1963) 201–251; T. S. Pattie, "An Unrecorded Greek Lectionary," JTS 18 (1967) 140–142; F. H. A. Scrivener, *A Plain Introduction to the Criticism of the New Testament*, 4th ed. (1894) vol. I, ch. 3, pp. 80–87: *Appendix*, "Synaxarion and Eclogadion of the Gospels and Apostolic Writings Daily Throughout the Year." See also the numerous studies in the University of Chicago series, *Studies in the Lectionary Text of the Greek New Testament*, vols. 1ff (University of Chicago 1933ff), on which see A. Wikgren, "Chicago Studies in the Greek Lectionary of the New Testament," in J. Neville Birdsall & R. Thomson (eds.), *Biblical and Patristic Studies in Memory of R. P. Casey* (Freiburg 1963) 96–121, who lists the volumes up to that date. These studies, along with several articles and yet unpublished PhD dissertations on the lectionary, deal principally with establishing the Greek text of the NT according to the lectionary tradition.

On the Prophetologion or Old Testament Lectionary, see: S. G. Engberg, "The Greek Old Testament Lectionary as a Liturgical Book," *Université de Copenhague, Cahiers de l'Institut du Moyen-âge grec et latin* 54 (1986) 39–48 (I am grateful to Prof. Peter Jeffery of the University of Delaware, who first brought this article to my attention and kindly sent me a photocopy of it); C. Hoeg, G. Zuntz (eds.), *Prophetologium*, MMB, Lectionaria I.1:1–6 (Copenhagen 1939–1970), II.1–2, ed. S. G. Engberg (1980–1981); C. Hoeg, G. Zuntz, "Remarks on the Prophetologion," in R. P. Casey, S. Lake, A. K. Lake (eds.), *Quantulacumque*.

Studies Presented to K. Lake (London 1937) 189–226; A. Rahlfs, "Die alttestamentlichen Lektionen der griechischen Kirche," *Nachrichten der kgl. Gesellschaft der Wissenschaften zu Göttingen, philologisch-historische Klasse* (1915) 28–136; G. Zuntz, "Das byzantinische Septuaginta-Lektionar ('Prophetologion')," *Classica et Mediaevalia* 17 (1956) 183–198.

To this already long list one can add several art-history studies on the illustrated Byzantine lectionary manuscripts.

18. Overview and further bibliography in Taft, *Beyond East and West;* also id., *Great Entrance;* id., "The Liturgy of the Great Church;" Mateos, *Célébration;* Schulz.

19. M. Arranz, "Sacrements" I–II–III (continuing).

20. See Taft, "Bibliography," esp. nos. 48–60, 80–81, 104, to which add the recent anthology of the prayers of this office by S. L. Parenti, *Il Signore della gloria. Preghiere della "Grande Chiesa" byzantina,* Preghiere di tutti i tempi 10 (Milan 1988) = id., *Praying with the Orthodox Tradition,* trans. P. Clifford (London 1989).

21. See Dagron, "Les moines," 231–232, 235–236; Taft, "Bibliography," nos. 3, 9, 19, 24–26, 79.

22. This is the topic of our next chapter.

23. Taft, "Liturgy."

24. The prayer is cited above in the final section of chapter 3.

25. I cite Germanus according to the chapter numbers of the text in P. Meyendorff, *Germanus;* but the translations are mine, from Taft, "Liturgy," done before Meyendorff published his version.

26. Apropos of this, see the remarks of Mango, "Mosaics," 48, on the three principles of Byzantine church decoration: hierarchical arrangement, selectivity, and explicitness, as crystallized in the "classical system" by the end of the ninth century. Mango writes, "The principle of explicitness was, in a sense, the repudiation of symbolism. . . . At the very end of the seventh century the Quinisext Council, in its famous Canon 82, prohibited the representation of Christ in the guise of a lamb. Instead of the symbol (*typos*), the anthropomorphic representation was to prevail. . . . The entire Iconoclastic controversy may be regarded, in this context, as the struggle between the symbol (the cross, favorite emblem of the Iconoclasts, being the *typos par excellence*), and the realistic image or *eikon.* In 843 the issue was further clarified in the so-called Synodikon of Orthodoxy. . . . In other words, Byzantine religious art of the ninth century demanded realism, not symbolism."

27. J. D. Mansi, *Sacrorum conciliorum nova et amplissima collectio* 13:264; Mango, *Art* 166.

5 The Studite Era

The period from about 800 until the Latin conquest of 1204–1261 was largely an age of recovery and consolidation in the Byzantine Empire. There were low as well as high points during this era. An initial period of renaissance under the Macedonians was succeeded in 1071 by collapse on the frontiers, as Norman and Seljuk victories led to the permanent loss of Italy and lay Asia Minor open to the Turks. There followed a partial revival under the Comnenoi in 1081–1204.

For the Church, shaken by a century of Iconoclasm and by increasing East-West conflict and estrangement, this period saw a greater subjugation of the patriarchate to the imperial power and the greater monasticization of ecclesiastical and liturgical life.[1] The defeat of Iconoclasm in 843, basically a monastic victory, had contributed to the demoralization of the secular clergy and a sharp rise in monastic influence: it was only during the iconoclastic struggle and its aftermath that monks came to play a dominant role in the hierarchy of the Orthodox Church and in the history of its liturgy.[2] This was largely due to the leadership of St. Theodore, abbot of Stoudios (d. 826), who in 799 led his monks out of Sakkoudion in Bithynia to the security of the capital.[3] There they found refuge in the dying, fifth-century Monastery of Stoudios, which they soon revivified, inaugurating the era of the Studite reform.[4]

The Victory of Orthodoxy and Liturgical Reform

Recent advances in the study of Byzantine Euchology manuscripts confirm that Iconoclasm was a major turning point in

Byzantine liturgical history.[5] The Byzantine Euchology or Prayerbook contains the prayers used by liturgical presiders—bishops or presbyters—at every sort of liturgical service. Its closest western parallel would be the Sacramentary. Like the old Roman Sacramentaries, the Euchology was not one uniform book: no two Euchology manuscripts are the same. Ongoing studies in the Euchology, especially by my colleague Miguel Arranz, S.J.,[6] and doctoral students under his direction at the Pontifical Oriental Institute in Rome, are gradually elaborating a more nuanced taxonomy of these Euchology manuscripts.[7] These studies confirm and develop criteria previously advanced by scholars such as the late Dom Anselm Strittmatter, O.S.B., of St. Anselm's Abbey in Washington, and André Jacob. These pioneers first distinguished various families and redactions of Euchology manuscripts, and Constantinopolitan sources from those of the Byzantine "liturgical periphery"[8]—chiefly the monastic centers of Southern Italy and Mt. Sinai before the predominance of Mt. Athos in the later period.[9]

This typology, especially as elaborated by Parenti, identifies an "old" or pre-iconoclastic "proto-formulary" extant only in manuscripts from Palestine/Sinai and Southern Italy, the latter characterized by oriental interpolations.[10] This pre-iconoclastic form traces its heritage back to earlier, now lost sources of the Constantinopolitan tradition, elements of which can be identified in the existing manuscripts. Later, beginning with the Studite Era, a new redaction of the Euchology emerged. Parenti calls this a "post-iconoclastic Euchology" in three separate traditions (Constantinopolitan,[11] Italo-Greek, Byzantino-Palestinian) and several distinct types (cathedral, parochial, monastic, mixed; pontifical or presbyteral), depending on their liturgical use.[12]

Certain characteristics common to these varieties of the "new Euchology" provide growing evidence of a liturgical reform initiated at Constantinople after the Victory of Orthodoxy in 843. This reform gradually spread to the periphery where, as has occurred at other times in the history of the liturgy, the reform was more conservative: changes were introduced more slowly while some elements of the old Euchology were stubbornly retained, and local peculiarities were not completely abandoned. The extant manuscript evidence shows that Palestine, with monastic centers in intensive contact with the Studite monasteries of the capital during the iconoclastic struggle and its aftermath, adopted the changes almost immediately. Southern Italy adopted such changes only gradually before the eleventh century, after which the changes were felt more strongly even there.[13] Though Parenti rightly calls this a true liturgical reform,[14] it was a gradual one, more analogous to the liturgical changes of the Roman Rite initiated under Pius X and continuing at increasing tempo throughout the long pontificate of Pius XII until Vatican II, than to the planned and expeditiously implemented overall reform set in motion by that council.

The Byzantine liturgical reform began, apparently, with the victory over Iconoclasm, during the brief patriarchate of St. Methodius I (4 March 843 to 14 June 847), to whose authorship are attributed several orthros canons and *idiomela* or festive refrains with their own melody, as well as rites of betrothal, nuptials, and second marriages.[15] Most important for our purposes, however, is another liturgical innovation: the *Diataxis for Converts of Diverse Ages and Circumstances*, composed, it seems, by Methodius himself. Popularly known as "The Diataxis of Methodius," this new rite for the reconciliation of apostates became one of distinguishing characteristics of the "new Euchology."[16]

Methodius, born in Syracuse, became a monk and hegumen in Bithynia in Northwest Asia Minor, across the Bosporus and Propontis from Constantinople and Thrace. He was the "restoration" patriarch following the deposition of the last iconoclastic patriarch, the learned John VIII Grammaticus, in 843, signalling the end of an era.[17] The iconodule "Victory of Orthodoxy," celebrated forever thereafter on "The Sunday of Orthodoxy"—the first Sunday of Lent in the Byzantine Calendar—was inaugurated, in typical Constantinopolitan fashion, with a stational procession to Hagia Sophia from the Church of the Theotokos in Blachernai, the iconodule stronghold in the capital. Accompanying Patriarch Methodius and the iconodule clergy in the procession and solemn entry into Hagia Sophia to take possession of the cathedral from the heretics, were the devout iconophile Empress Theodora (842–846) and her imperial retinue, including her trusted advisor the eunuch Theoktistos, who had orchestrated the felicitous denouement.[18]

Of greater liturgical significance than the Diataxis of Methodius or the Sunday of Orthodoxy, were the lasting reforms in the eucharist of the Great Church enacted in this same period. A new redaction of the Liturgy of St. John Chrysostom, comprising emendations in the anaphoral text—chiefly stylistic revisions and assimilations to the Anaphora of St. Basil—had already emerged by the turn of the millennium.[19] This new redaction of the Chrysostom liturgy ultimately replaced the Liturgy of St. Basil as the principal eucharistic formulary of the Byzantine Church. The Liturgy of St. Basil was gradually relegated, in the mobile cycle, to the Sundays of Lent, Holy Thursday, the Holy Saturday Easter Vigil; in the fixed cycle, it was employed on the feast of St. Basil (January 1) and the vigils of Christmas and Theophany, unless they fell on Saturday or Sunday, in which case the Liturgy of St. Basil was celebrated on the feast itself.[20] Gregor Hanke, O.S.B., preparing a study on the Divine Office according to the Rite of the Great Church, has also noted changes around this time in manuscripts of the Byzantine Liturgical Psalter.[21] There, as in the Euchology, old and new redactions continued in use side by side from the ninth until the end of the eleventh century, and sources show the strain of those who were for and those who were against the changes.[22] Only by the turn of the twelfth-thirteenth century did the new redaction by and large win out.

In spite of these changes, from a liturgical point of view, surprising as it may seem, the cathedral/parochial liturgy of Byzantium was far more conservative than the monastic Office. The changes in the Euchology initiated at this time were more a question of fine tuning than a major overhaul. Thus Arranz can affirm that, between the eighth and the fourteenth centuries, "the liturgy of Constantinople changed but little."[23] Consequent to the reform one notes what Parenti has called a strong tendency to "orational atrophy": many more prayers fall into disuse than are replaced by any new liturgical creativity, though local peculiarities continue to emerge on the periphery.

The Development of the Monastic Rite: A Tale of Two Cities

In the Studite monasteries, liturgical creativity, fueled by the fierce monastic opposition to Iconoclasm, was proceeding apace. We have already noted changes in the Liturgical Psalter. They were the direct result of the growing monasticization of the Orthodox Church in the post-iconoclastic period. Despite the numerous problems the Studite monks encountered from the new patriarch Methodius, who was too easy on the former Iconoclasts for their tastes,[24] the victory over Iconoclasm left the monks of Constantinople in an advantageous position vis-à-vis the secular clergy. Monasteries became richer, more autonomous and more numerous especially in urban areas. After the Early Byzantine Period, far more monastic than secular churches were built.[25]

As for the liturgy, the remainder of the history of the Byzantine Rite, if less significant for the *histoire des mentalités*, reflects this symbiosis of cathedral and monastery: first as an ongoing "Tale of Two Cities": Constantinople and Jerusalem,[26] then as a "Tale of Two Monastic 'Deserts'," Palestine and Mount Athos, as the story moves toward its denouement in the hesychast synthesis of the fourteenth century.[27]

I call it an ongoing tale, for this is not its beginning but its continuation. Even before the period under discussion here, as the liturgy of Constantinople was being influenced by Palestinian usages, a gradual byzantinization of hagiopolite liturgy was also underway: a process fostered, undoubtedly, by the predominance of the Patriarchate of Constantinople throughout the East from the end of Late Antiquity. According to Dmitrievskij, before the seventh century it was Jerusalem that held liturgical sway, exerting its influence on Constantinople. From the first half of the seventh century, however, the influence became mutual, with Constantinople a source as well as recipient of liturgical diffusion. This continued in the post-iconoclastic period, when the Great Church emerged from the debacle victorious, with renewed unity and strength. By the turn of the millennium the tide was reversed, with Constantinople henceforth dominating the periphery liturgically.[28]

The earliest extant manuscript of the Jerusalem eucharistic Liturgy of St. James, the ninth-century roll *Vatican Gr. 2282*,[29] shows unmistakable traces of this byzantinization already well underway. Indeed, throughout this period the liturgical byzantinization of the Orthodox Patriarchates of Alexandria, Antioch, and Jerusalem, weakened successively by Monophysitism, the Islamic conquests, and the Crusades, proceeded apace. It was fostered especially by Theodore IV Balsamon, absentee Patriarch of Antioch (1186–1203), resident in Constantinople.[30] By the end of the thirteenth century, the process was more or less complete in Alexandria and Antioch, though the Liturgy of James remained in use longer in the Patriarchate of Jerusalem, and Greek manuscripts of the non-Byzantine Melkite liturgies continue to be copied until the end of Byzantium.[31]

More important for the history of the Byzantine Rite was its internal evolution: not how the Rite of Constantinople ultimately supplanted other Orthodox Rites, but rather how one of them, the Rite of Jerusalem, affected the Rite of Constantinople. However, this too depended on external circumstances. By this time the stage had already shifted to the monasteries: first of Palestine and Constantinople, then, in the fourteenth century, to Mt. Athos.[32] Although all aspects of this interaction are far from clear, its broad outlines may be summarized as follows.

After the first phase of the iconoclastic crisis (726–787), while all of the already developed rites of the Great Church continued in use even after the empire had slid into its Dark Ages, the seeds of a new spring were already germinating in the monasteries of the Studite confederation. By the time of the Studite reform, the new representational view of liturgy had already taken hold, and the Studite reform leader St. Theodore adopted it without reserve:

> Do you not think that the divine myron is to be regarded as a type of Christ, the divine table as his lifegiving tomb, the linen as that in which he was buried, the lance of the priest as that which pierced his side, and the sponge as that in which he received the drink of vinegar? Set all these aside, and what will be left to render present the divine mysteries?[33]

These are borrowed views, however, and Theodore's central place in the history of Byzantine worship lies not in his adoption of the current outlook, but on a far more pragmatic level. His interest was in the defeat of Iconoclasm and in monastic reform. This is why he summoned to Stoudios some monks of the Monastery of St. Sabas in the Judean Desert between Jerusalem and the Dead Sea, a fateful decision fraught with consequences for the future history of the Byzantine Rite.

St. Sabas had itself undergone a remarkable renaissance in the restoration following the Persian onslaught of 614. It was from this rebirth that the explosion of Sabaitic liturgical poetry dates, chants that Theodore considered a sure guide of orthodoxy in the struggle against the heretics.[34] It was this office of St. Sabas, not the *Akolouthia ton Akoimeton* or "Office of the Sleepless Monks" then current in the monasteries of the capital, that the Studites synthesized with material from the *Asmatike Akolouthia* or cathedral office of the Great Church to create the hybrid Studite office: a Palestinian Horologion with its psalmody and hymnody grafted onto a skeleton of litanies and prayers from the Euchology of the Great Church.

Originally scattered in disparate collections of *kanones, stichera, kontakaria, tropologia, kathismata,* this new poetry eventually was codified in the later Byzantine anthologies of propers for the daily (Oktoechos: 8th c.[35]), lenten-paschal (Triodion: 10th c.), and fixed (Menaion: 10th c.) cycles of the liturgical year, in that order, beginning in the centuries indicated.[36] As this material came together, creating an interference of competing cycles, the need to direct the increased traffic was felt. So at the beginning of the second millennium a new type of monastic book, the developed Typikon, began to appear, to regulate the interference of these three conflicting cycles of the proper.[37]

Earlier, first-generation Studite Typika, like the western *Rule of St. Benedict*,[38] are little more than monastic rules with rudimentary liturgical regulations. But those liturgical regulations are clearly Studite, and this usage quickly spread from Constantinople to other Orthodox monastic centers. The foundational hagiorite rule on Mt. Athos, the *Hypotyposis of Athanasius of the Great Lavra,* written by Athanasius himself soon after the foundation of the Great Lavra in 962–963, is but a slight retouching of the *Hypotyposis of Stoudios.*[39]

This Studite-type Typikon grew in liturgical detail as the synthesis of Sabaitic and Constantinopolitan practices progressed, and spread far and wide. The first such developed Studite Typikon was composed by Alexis, hegumen of Stoudios and later patriarch of Constantinople from 1025–1043, for the monastery he founded near the capital. It was this Typikon, now extant only in six Slavonic manuscripts,[40] that St. Theodosius Pecherskij translated into Slavonic in the eleventh century and introduced as the rule of the Kievo-Pecherskaya Lavra or Monastery of the Caves in Kiev, cradle of Orthodox monasticism among the East Slavs. From Ukraine it passed to the whole of Rus' and Muscovy.[41]

By the beginning of the twelfth century, the developed Studite synthesis had also appeared in Magna Graecia, in full form, in the Typikon of San Salvatore of Messina (A.D. 1131).[42] It surfaced on Mt. Athos at Iviron in the Typikon of George III Mt'acmindeli (ca. 1009–d. 29 June 1065), that is, "the Hagiorite,"[43] eighth hegumen of Iviron from ca. 1044 until his resignation in 1065. His Typikon, based on a Constantinopolitan Greek original that dates from before 906, was translated into Georgian between 1042 and 1044, before George's abbacy. It is extant in several Georgian manuscripts, the earliest of which are from the eleventh century.[44] This key document, the first full description of liturgical life on Mt. Athos, shows that the earliest hagiorite liturgy followed Studite usage, which by that time was already an amalgam of Sabaitic uses—*Phos hilaron* at vespers, Palestinian orthros (matins), with canon, etc.—with the Rite of the Great Church.[45]

This fusion, completed by the twelfth century, added to the

more sober, desert prayer of Palestinian monasticism a ritual solemnity giving it what Arranz calls "a strong Byzantine coloration, a certain taste for the cathedral tradition, an importance assigned to chant to the detriment of the psalter. . . ."[46] All of these would become permanent characteristics of the Byzantine Liturgy of the Hours.

By the twelfth century this Studite rite—which Arranz calls "the tradition of the Byzantine West" to distinguish it from the "oriental" or Palestinian neo-Sabaitic synthesis—was found on Athos and in Rus', Georgia, and Southern Italy.

The New Holy Week and Easter Services

Part and parcel of this same, largely monastic, interchange was the gradual formation of the Byzantine Holy Week and Easter Vigil rites: also a synthesis of elements from the usages of Jerusalem and the Great Church which began in this period and was only completed in the next.[47]

Church Music

The changes introduced in this period were reflected in every aspect of Byzantine church life. Musicologist Oliver Strunk, for instance, noted the same process in the sources of his discipline. In Constantinople one sees at first the two traditions, cathedral and monastic, as parallel but independent, with the cathedral easily preeminent. Then, as they influence each other, the monastic rite gradually assumes the lead, becoming predominant in the eleventh century.[48] Dimitri Conomos discerned the same dialectic in his study of the Late Byzantine *koinonika* or communion chants.[49] In the earliest extant Byzantine musical manuscripts there were initially two independent traditions: a monastic chant tradition, and the remains of an early, uniform, archetypal congregational melody.[50] These two streams originally went their own way, but their intermingling can be observed by the middle of the eleventh century in the Triodion codex *Vatopedi 1488* (ca. 1050) and in codex *Grottaferrata Gb 35* (ca. 1100).[51]

Church Architecture and Iconography

More perceptible on the concrete level of popular piety were the changes in the architecture, decoration, and liturgical disposition of the church. As Mathews has shown, every single characteristic of the original Constantinopolitan church arrangement changed after Iconoclasm. The most notable among them were the large, single-apse basilical style, with large atrium, narthex, and multiple, monumental external entrances on all sides, including the outside entrances to the galleries that surrounded the nave on all but the east or sanctuary side. Inside there was extraordinary openness of design, with no internal divisions, no side-apses, pastophoria, or auxiliary chambers anywhere on the ground floor (the skeuophylakion or sacristy was in a separate building outside). The sanctuary chancel barrier was of open design: all was visible within. Indeed, as if to assure this, the altar stood in front of the apse, not inside it, for the apse was taken up by the throne and synthronon, raised on several steps so that the presiding clergy could easily be seen. The monumental ambo occupied the center of the nave, often joined to the open chancel by the solea pathway. And the decoration, generally in mosaic, was sparse to the extreme.

The often miniscule post-iconoclastic church turned inward: without atrium or monumental entrances; the altar retreating within the new, triple-apsed, enclosed sanctuary; small enough to be frescoed over every inch of its interior surface; too small to hold galleries, monumental ambo, solea, elevated synthronon; no longer needing a skeuophylakion since the gifts are now prepared in the new prothesis or side-apse to the northeast side. Such a provincial-style church building could not be more different than its pre-iconoclastic predecessors in the capital.[52]

New Euchology, new Typikon, new Divine Office, new liturgical music, new iconography, new architecture and liturgical arrangement of the church, new mystagogy to interpret it all: the Middle-Byzantine synthesis is complete.

Notes

1. On Byzantine monasticism, see Taft, "Bibliography," nos. 1–28, to which add C. Capizzi, "Origine e sviluppo del monachesimo nell' area di Costantinopoli fino a Giustiniano," in *Storia europea. Il monachesimo nel primo millennio*. Convegno internazionale di studi, Roma, 24–25 febbraio 1989, Casamari, 26 febbraio 1989. Atti (Rome 1989) 79–97.

2. See H.-G. Beck, *Das byzantinische Jahrtausend* (Munich 1978) 210–11. Though a history of monasticism in Constantinople remains to be written, the basic study on the origins and early role of the monks is Dagron, "Les moines." On the condition of the secular clergy in the Middle and Late Byzantine Periods, see, for example, C. Cupane, "Una 'classe sociale' dimenticata: il basso clero metropolitano," in H. Hunger (ed.), *Studien zum Patriarchatsregister von Konstantinopel*, Österreichischen Akademie der Wissenschaften, phil.-hist. Klasse, Sitzungsberichte 383 (Vienna 1981) I, 66–79; L. Oeconomos, "L'état intellectuel et moral des byzantins vers le milieu du XIVe siècle d'aprés une page de Joseph Bryennios," in *Mélanges Charles Diehl* (Paris 1930) I, 225–233; Nicol 98ff.

3. A contemporary study of Theodore's life and work is badly needed. Meanwhile, two older studies, though very outdated, remain useful: A. P. Dobroklonskij, *Prepodobnyj Fedor, ispovednik i igumen studijskij*, I. Chast': *Ego epoxa, zhizn', i dejatel'nost'* (Odessa 1913); II. Chast': *Ego tvorenija*. Vypusk 1 (Odessa 1914); Alice Gardner, *Theodore of Studium. His Life and Times* (London 1905).

4. Stoudios, founded in 463, was a daughter house of the *akoimetoi* monks discussed in the previous chapter at note 21: Dagron, "Les moines," 236 and note 46. For studies on the Studite reform, see Taft, "Bibliography," 358–359.

5. Arranz, "Sacrements" I.1, OCP 48 (1982) 322–323; Taft, "Liturgy," 46, 72.

6. In addition to his series of fifteen articles on the Hours and other offices in the Constantinopolitan Euchology in OCP 37 (1971)–48 (1982), and other occasional studies on the topic, all listed in Taft, "Bibliography," nos. 29–30, 49–61, 157, and id., "Mt. Athos," 180 note 7; see Arranz, "Euchologe slave;" id., "Sacrements" I-II-III.

7. See, for example, the remarks in Arranz, "Euchologe slave," 21–23; id., "Sacrements" I.1: OCP 48 (1982) 330–335; Parenti, "Influssi," 153ff; id., *L'Eucologio manoscritto Gb IV (X secolo) della Biblioteca di Grottaferrata. Edizione* (doctoral dissertation in preparation at the Pontifical Oriental Institute under the direction of M. Arranz); Thiermeyer, *Ottoboni gr. 434*, 85ff; Stephan J. Koster, *Das Euchologion Sevastianov 474 (X/XI Jhdt.) der Staatsbibliothek Lenin in Moskau* (unpublished doc-

toral dissertation under the direction of M. Arranz, 1991) 25ff. In addition, I owe my thanks to S. Parenti for numerous valuable suggestions concerning this chapter, esp. on the nature and history of the Euchology.

8. The expression is S. Parenti's. Relevant essential bibliography of Strittmatter and Jacob in Parenti, "Osservazioni," 146-148.

9. Cf. Taft, "Mt. Athos."

10. Parenti, "Osservazioni" and "Influssi;" cf. also id., "Tradizione liturgica dell'Italia meridionale bizantina," *L'altra Europa* XIV = 5 [227] (settembre-ottobre 1989) 41-55 (continuing); Jacob, "Tradition;" Taft, *Great Entrance* xxxii.

11. A classic example is the patriarchal Euchology of the Great Church in codex *Paris Coislin 213* (A.D. 1027) referred to above, ch. 4, note 11.

12. Parenti, "Influssi," 153-155; id., "Osservazioni," 151-153; and personal communications; Thiermeyer, *Ottoboni gr. 434*, 85-94.

13. Parenti, "Osservazioni," 151-153.

14. Ibid. 151; Parenti, "Influssi," 173-174.

15. His works and their mss are listed in J. B. Pitra, *Iuris ecclesiastici Graecorum historia et monumenta* (Rome 1868) II, 353-355. I owe this reference to my student S. Parenti.

16. Ibid. 354 lists twenty-four mss containing the Diataxis, on which see M. Arranz, "La 'Diataxis' du Patriarche Méthode pour la réconciliation des apostats," OCP 56 (1990) 283-322; id., "Circonstances et conséquences liturgiques du Concile de Ferrare-Florence," in G. Alberigo (ed.), *Christian Unity. The Council of Ferrare-Florence 1438/39-1989*, Bibliotheca Ephemeridum Theologicarum Lovaniensium 97 (Louvain 1991) 425; cf. also id., "Sacrements" I.10, OCP 55 (1989) 318-319 note 2; id., "Evolution des rites d'incorporation et de réadmission dans l'Église selon l'Euchologe byzantin," in *Gestes et paroles dans les diverses familles liturgiques*, BELS 14 (Rome 1978) 31-75, here 50-51, 71ff; id., "Euchologe slave," 40-42.

17. On Methodius see Pitra (note 15 above) 351-365; V. Grumel, "La politique religieuse du patriarche saint Méthode. Iconoclastes et studites," *Echos d'orient* 34 (1935) 385-401; A. Kazhdan, "Methodios I," ODB 2:1355.

18. Cf. J. Gouillard, "Le Synodikon de l'Orthodoxie. Édition et commentaire," *Travaux et mémoires* 2 (1967) 120-129; P. A. Hollingsworth, "Theoktistos," ODB 3:2056; id. with A. Kazhdan & A. Cutler, "Triumph of Orthodoxy," ODB 3:2122-2123; Pitra (note 15 above) 351.

19. Thorough analysis and relevant bibliography in Parenti, "Osservazioni"; cf. also Taft, *Great Entrance* xxxi-xxxiv.

20. Other elements of the reform in Thiermeyer, *Ottoboni gr. 434*, 88-89.

21. Private communication; cf. Thiermeyer, *Ottoboni gr. 434*, 92.

22. My student A.-A. Thiermeyer shows this in his forthcoming study, "Diataxis des Codex Barberini gr. 316," in preparation.

23. "Euchologe slave," 23.

24. See Grumel, "La politique," (note 17 above); J. Darrouzès, "Le patriarche Méthode contre les iconoclastes et les Stoudites," *Revue des études byzantines* 45 (1987) 15–57; I. Doens, Ch. Hannick, "Das Periorismos-Dekret des Patriarchen Methodios I. gegen die Studiten Naukratios und Athanasios," JöB 22 (1983) 93–102.

25. Mango, *Architecture* 197–198 and ch. 7–8 passim.

26. I illustrate this in Taft, "A Tale of Two Cities"; id., "Paschal Triduum."

27. I detail these later developments in Taft, "Mt. Athos."

28. Cf. A. A. Dmitrievskij, *Drevnejshie patriarshie tipikony: Svjatogrobskij, Ierusalimskij i Velikoj Konstantinopol'skoj Tserkvi* (Kiev 1907), ch. 3; A. Baumstark, "Denkmäler der Entstehungsgeschichte des byzantinischen Ritus," OC series 3, vol. 2 (1927) 1–32; id., "Die Heiligtümer des byzantinischen Jerusalems nach einer übersehenen Urkunde," OC 5 (1905) 227–289, esp. 282–89; R. Taft, "A Proper Offertory Chant for Easter in Some Slavonic Manuscripts," OCP 36 (1970) 440–42; Thiermeyer, *Ottoboni gr. 434*, 91.

29. B.-Ch. Mercier (ed.), *La Liturgie de S. Jacques. Édition critique, avec traduction latine*, Patrologia Orientalis 26.2 (Paris 1946) 115–256 (H in the apparatus).

30. See PG 137:621; 138:953.

31. The history of this development remains to be written. See, however, J. Nasrallah, "La liturgie des Patriarcats melchites de 969 à 1300," OC 71 (1987) 156–181; and the still useful earlier studies of C. Korolevsky (Karalevsky), *Histoire des patriarcats melkites (Alexandrie, Antioche, Jérusalem) depuis le schisme monophysite du sixième siècle jusqu'à nos jours*, II–III (Rome 1910–1911) I, 5–9, 12–21; id. (C. Charon), "Le rite byzantin et la liturgie chrysostomienne dans les patriarcats melkites (Alexandrie-Antioche-Jérusalem)," *XPYCOCTOMIKA. Studi e ricerche intorno a S. Giovanni Crisostomo*, a cura del comitato per il XVº centenario della sua morte, 407–1907 (Rome 1908) 473–497; P. de Meester, "Grecques (liturgies)," *Dictionnaire d'archéologie chrétien et de liturgie* VI.2:1605–1608.

32. See Taft, "Mt. Athos."

33. *Kephalaia adv. iconomachos* 1, PG 99:489B, English trans. from Schulz 62.

34. *Ep. II*, 15-16, PG 99:1160-1168.

35. Mss begin to unify this material for Sundays from the 8th c., but the name "Oktoechos" first appears in the 11th c. I am grateful to my student Elena Velkovska for referring me to the earliest Menaion mss.

36. See my articles under the names of these books in ODB.

37. On the Typikon, see Taft, "Bibliography," nos. 29–47; to which add my ODB articles: "Typikon, Liturgical"; "Typikon of the Great Church"; "Stoudite Typika"; "Sabaitic Typika"; A. Skaf, "Typika," *Dictionnaire de spiritualité* 15 (Paris 1991) 1358–1371; and esp. the work of my student Abraham-Andreas Thiermeyer, "Das Typikon-Ktetorikon und sein literarhistorischer Kontext," forthcoming in OCP. This study, from Thiermeyer's 1990 Licentiate Thesis written under my direction at the Pontifical Oriental Institute, Rome, gives the most thorough available analysis and typology of the Typikon, including a complete list of the known extant Typika, published and unpublished and, for the former, where they have been edited.

38. On the liturgical code in early Latin monastic rules, see Taft, *Hours*, chs. 6–7.

39. In their present redaction the earliest Studite rules, the *Hypotyposis of Stoudios* and the *Hypotyposis of Athanasius of the Great Lavra*, date, respectively, from the generation after St. Theodore (d. 826) and St. Athanasius, who died in the first years of the eleventh century: on all these documents see Taft, "Mt. Athos," 182–184.

40. The mss are listed in D. Petras, *The Typicon of the Patriarch Alexis the Studite: Novgorod-St. Sophia 1136*, excerpt from a doctoral dissertation at the Pontifical Oriental Institute under the direction of M. Arranz (Cleveland 1991) 9–10, that studies and gives a partial translation of the third oldest ms, the 13th c. codex *Novgorod St. Sophia 1136*.

41. Taft, "Mt. Athos," 184.

42. Arranz, *Typicon*.

43. from Mt'acminda or "The Holy Mountain."

44. Full documentation in Taft, "Mt. Athos," 185–6, to which add the recent study on Iviron in one of George's writings: B. Martin-Hisard, "*La Vie de Jean et Euthyme* et le statut du monastère des Ibères sur l'Athos," *Revue des études byzantines* 49 (1991) 67–142.

45. Taft, "Mt. Athos," 186.

46. Arranz, "Matines," OCP 38 (1972) 85.

47. S. Janeras, *Le Vendredi-saint dans la tradition liturgique byzantine. Structure et histoire de ses offices*, AL 12 = SA 99 (Rome 1988) and my review of the same in OCP 56 (1990) 227–29; G. Bertonière, *The Historical Development of the Easter Vigil and Related Services in the Greek Church*, OCA 193 (Rome 1972) passim, esp. 279–301; Taft, "Paschal Triduum;" id., "A Tale of Two Cities."

48. Strunk, *Music* 137 and passim.

49. See Conomos, *Communion Cycle*, and my reviews of the same in OCP 54 (1988) 244–246, and *Worship* 62 (1988) 554–557.

50. Conomos, *Communion Cycle, passim*, esp. 65–71.

51. Ibid. 67, citing E. Follieri, O. Strunk (eds.), *Triodium Athoum*, MMB, Series principalis IX.1-2 (Copenhagen 1975); O. Strunk (ed.), *Specimena notationum antiquiorum*, MMB, Series principalis VII (Copenhagen 1966) plates 34–42.

52. Mathews, *passim*, esp. ch. 4; Taft, *Great Entrance* 179–191.

6 The Middle-Byzantine Synthesis

If the Middle-Byzantine synthesis represents a change over what went before in the Early-Byzantine period,[1] I do not for a moment wish to imply that it was not in full continuity with the Orthodox tradition. The same theology is at the basis of Byzantine mystagogy and icon worship in post-iconoclastic Byzantium. And as we noted in chapter 3, both dimensions of this theology—church building and liturgy as a mirror of the mysteries of salvation, church building and liturgy as cosmic and eschatological images of the heavenly realm and its worship—had already emerged ca. 730 in Germanus' commentary on the liturgy and on the church where the mysteries were reenacted.

One may debate eternally whether the chicken came before the egg, and my point is not to prove a causal nexus (though I believe there to be one) between the iconodule theory of religious images on the one hand, and the more representational mystagogy of the liturgical anamnesis and its concomitant decorative programs on the other. But all three gained the upper hand in Byzantine theology and art about the same time and represent, in my view, the victory of monastic popular devotion over a more spiritualist and symbolic approach to liturgy.[2]

The New Iconography

If theological interpretation of the new spirituality was canonized in liturgical commentaries, it could be communicated to the masses only through the ritual celebration and its setting: through the liturgical disposition and decoration of the church building, as it evolved in Byzantine churches at the turn of the tenth-eleventh centuries, during the Studite era treated in the previous chapter.

There is evidence for representational church decoration in Late Antique Palestine before this period. The early sixth-century rhetorician Choricius of Gaza described the St. Sergius Church in Gaza, probably built before 536, as fully frescoed with over twenty-five scenes of Jesus' life from the Annunciation to the Ascension.[3] But Gaza is not Constantinople, and the earliest witness to such a decorative program—still embryonic, as there is no mention of a festive cycle—in the Rite of the Great Church is Patriarch Photius (858–867, 877–886), who described the mosaics of the Church of the Virgin of the Pharos, the palatine chapel or principal sanctuary of the Imperial Palace.

> On the very ceiling is painted in colored mosaic cubes a man-like figure bearing the traits of Christ. You might say He is overseeing the earth, and devising its orderly arrangement and government, so accurately has the painter been inspired to represent, though only in forms and colors, the Creator's care for us. In the concave segments next to the summit of the hemisphere a throng of angels is pictured escorting our common Lord. The apse which rises over the sanctuary glistens with the image of the Virgin, stretching out her stainless arms on our behalf and winning for the emperor safety and exploits against the foes. A choir of apostles and martyrs, yea, of prophets too, and patriarchs fill and beautify the whole church with their images . . .[4]

Previously, witnesses may have assigned symbolic meaning to various parts of the Constantinopolitan church building,[5] and there was some representational art in Hagia Sophia.[6] But the use of extensive representational art programs began in Constantinople only in the Middle Byzantine Period, following the final defeat of Iconoclasm in 843, when an iconographic program was elaborated to express this vision to those unreached by the literary productions of a Germanus.[7]

These programs reflect the two-tiered symbolism of the new mystagogy we saw in Germanus: [1] the cosmic, "heavenly-liturgy" vision inherited from Maximus and, [2] the "economic" or anamnetic *historia* with its explicit, representational depiction of salvation history. In the cosmic or hierarchical scheme, church and ritual are an image of the present age of the Church, in which divine grace is mediated to those in the world (nave) from the divine abode (sanctuary) and its heavenly worship (the liturgy enacted there), which in turn images forth its future consummation (eschatological), when we shall enter that abode in glory. Symeon of Thessalonika (d. 1429), last of the classic Byzantine mystagogues, has synthesized this vision in chapter 131 of his treatise *On the Holy Temple:*

> The church, as the house of God, is an image of the whole world, for God is everywhere and above everything . . . The sanctuary is a symbol of the higher and super-celestial spheres, where the throne of God and his dwelling place are said to be. It is this throne which the altar represents. The heavenly hierarchies are found in many places, but here they are accompanied by priests who take their place. The bishop represents Christ, the church [nave] represents the visible world . . . Outside it are the lower regions and the world of beings that live not according to reason, and have no higher life. The sanctuary receives within itself the bishop, who represents the God-man Jesus whose almighty powers he shares. The other sacred ministers represent the apostles and especially the angels and archangels, each according to his order. I mention the apostles with the angels, bishops, and priests, because there is only one Church, above and below, since God came down and lived among us, doing what he was sent to do on our behalf. And it is a work which is one, as is our Lord's sacrifice, communion, and contemplation. And it is carried out both above and here below, but with this difference: above it is done without any veils or symbols, but here it is accomplished through symbols. . . .[8]

In the economic or anamnetic scheme, the sanctuary with its altar is at once: the Holy of Holies of the tabernacle decreed by Moses; the Cenacle of the Last Supper; Golgotha of the crucifixion; and the Holy Sepulchre of the resurrection, from which the sacred gifts of the Risen Lord—his Word and his body and blood—issue forth to illumine the sin-darkened world. This second level receives prominence in Germanus:

The church is heaven on earth, where the God of heaven dwells and moves. It images forth the crucifixion and burial and resurrection of Christ. It is glorified above the tabernacle of the testimony of Moses with its expiatory and holy of holies, prefigured in the patriarchs, founded on the apostles, adorned in the hierarchs, perfected in the martyrs . . . The holy altar stands for the place where Christ was laid in the grave, on which the true and heavenly bread, the mystical and bloodless sacrifice, lies, his flesh and blood offered to the faithful as the food of eternal life. It is also the throne of God on which the incarnate God reposes . . . and like the table at which he was in the midst of his disciples at his Mystical Supper . . . prefigured in the table of the Old Law where the manna was, which is Christ, come down from heaven.

In the iconography and liturgy of the church, this twofold vision assumes visible and dynamic form. From the central dome the image of the Pantocrator dominates the whole scheme, giving unity to the hierarchical and economic themes. The movement of the hierarchical theme is vertical: ascending from the present, worshipping community assembled in the nave, up through the ranks of the saints, prophets, patriarchs, and apostles, to the Lord in the heavens attended by the angelic choirs.[9] The economic or "salvation-history" system, extending outwards and upwards from the sanctuary, is united both artistically and theologically with the hierarchical.

Within this setting the liturgical community commemorates the mystery of its redemption in union with the worship of the Heavenly Church. It offers the mystery of Christ's covenant through the outstretched hands of his mother. All of this was made present to the unlettered in the sacrament of the iconographic scheme. Indeed, it is only in the actual liturgical celebration that the symbolism of the church comes alive, and appears as more than a static embodiment of the cosmos as seen through Christian eyes. In Christian belief, a dynamic link between the created and uncreated worlds was forged by Christ in the covenant of his blood—a covenant that the eucharist celebrates, ratifies, and renews. This dynamic bond is expressed in both the disposition and iconography of the church.

The iconostasis, enclosing the sanctuary wherein the mysteries of the covenant are celebrated, is conceived as the link between heaven and earth. Beyond and above the altar, on the wall of the central sanctuary apse, is depicted "The Communion of the Apostles." This is not the historic Last Supper, but Christ the heavenly High Priest, attended by the angels, giving the eucharist to the Twelve. Saints Basil and Chrysostom, whose liturgical formularies express the same mystery, may be found there too, holding liturgical scrolls, as if concelebrating the rites being performed before them on the heavenly/earthly altar. Over the altar, in the conch of the sanctuary apse, is the Theotokos. Her arms are outstretched in the orant position, as if interceding in our behalf and hastening, through her hands, our offering to the Pantocrator above her in the dome. With her, in the nimbus of her womb, is the Christ child, figure of the incarnation that made this sacrificial intercession possible, figure of Mary/Church as womb of God, bringing forth Jesus again and again in human hearts. Above this, at the summit of the sanctuary arch, is "The Throne of Divine Judgment," where the sacrificial mediation must intercede before God. Out from the sanctuary, frescoes of liturgical feasts depicting the Christian economy of salvation in Jesus extend around the walls of the church clockwise, in lateral bands like hoops around a barrel, binding the saving *historia* of the past into the salvific renewal of the present.[10]

The New Architecture

Since our focus is liturgy, I shall leave the decorative programs to the art historians. Note, however, that these programs were intimately related to changes in church architecture that were equally significant from a liturgical perspective. As Cyril Mango notes, such unitary decorative schemes were feasible only in the post-Justinianic period, when the entire cruciform, domed interior of much smaller churches "was visible at one glance (there were no aisles) so that it could be treated as a unit for purposes of decoration."[11] Such a radical change of venue and scale was brought about partly because of the socio-political and economic situation of the period. As a consequence of the "Dark Ages," the monumental architecture of the Justinianic period was succeeded by Middle and Late Byzantine churches often miniature by comparison. As churches became smaller, liturgical life became more compressed, more private. The splendors of the urban stational and basilical rites of Late Antiquity, destined for a liturgical space that encompassed the city, and tailored to the majestic dimensions of a Hagia Sophia, were henceforth played out in a greatly reduced arena.

The growing monasticization of the Constantinopolitan Patriarchate after Iconoclasm played a role in this development. Monasteries became richer, more autonomous and more powerful, especially the urban Studite monasteries in close contact with the secular churches. It is not an accident that in the later centuries of Byzantium, far more monastic than secular churches were built.[12] Monastic liturgy is not stational but cloistered, a stay-at-home liturgy confined to the buildings of the monastic complex.

A Reduced Ritual and its Symbolism

This compression of liturgical activity within the walls of ever-smaller church buildings was accompanied by a shift toward greater symbolization. When rites, once of practical import, outlive their original purpose, their continued survival demands reintegration into a new system. In the process, such relics often acquire new symbolic interpretations, unrelated to their genesis or original scope.

The classic example is, again, the introit procession at the beginning of the eucharistic liturgy. Originally this was a solemn entrance into the church, with strong longitudinal lines corresponding to the longitudinal axis of the early basilicas.[13] The new ritual, though still imposing, was confined within the much smaller, centrally planned churches. The once great public introit processions—reduced to ritual turns within the interior of a now tiny nave—became a truncated, clerical remnant of the original entrance of the entire church, as was recorded in the Italo-Greek Introit Prayer in some manuscripts of the Chrysostom Liturgy:

> Benefactor and artisan of all creation, receive the church which approaches. Bring about what is good for each of us, lead us to perfection, and make us worthy of your kingdom. . . .[14]

In the new system the two entrance processions, truncated to ritual appearances of the sacred ministers from behind the sanctuary barrier, perdure on a reduced scale, reinterpreted as epiphanies of Christ. In the first procession or Lesser Introit that opens the Liturgy of the Word, the Gospel book is borne out from the altar through the nave and back again. It is said to signify Christ's coming to us as Word. The Great Entrance or Major Introit at the beginning of the eucharistic half of the service was once, too, a functional entrance into the church from the outside skeuophylakion with the bread and wine prepared there before the liturgy. Reduced to a solemn transfer of the bread and wine from the Prothesis credence in the sanctuary, out through the nave, then back again to the sanctuary to be deposited on the altar, it is said to show Christ being led to his sacrifice, and to prefigure his coming to us in the sacrament of his body and blood. These foreshadowings are fulfilled in two later ritual appearances from behind the sanctuary chancel: the procession of the deacon with the Gospel lectionary for the reading, and the procession of the presiding celebrant to distribute the consecrated gifts in communion.

This move toward smaller scale also entailed a greater privatization of the liturgy. Not only are processions reduced to ritualized remnants of no practical import that end where they began; within the church itself, the ritual action withdraws to the ever more completely enclosed sanctuary. The proliferation of private oratories with their clergy are further signs of the shift away from monumental public services to the more domestic and monastic.[15]

Resulting Changes in Church Arrangement

The results of all this in the liturgical disposition of the church were multiple:[16]

1. the atrium vanished and the number of doorways was greatly reduced;

2. the outside skeuophylakion was abandoned, replaced by the pastophoria;

3. the elevated synthronon disappeared from the apse; and,

4. the great ambo was displaced from the middle of the nave, greatly reduced in size and moved off-center, or even removed entirely, as the proclamation of the Word became a ritualized formality; even preaching was usually reduced to the reading of a ready text from some homiliary.[17]

Retroinfluence of the New Interpretation on the Text

Not only were church buildings, iconography, and ritual affected in this process. Liturgies have both an inner and an outer history that interact dialectically. This is especially true in the Byzantine East, where the spiritual understanding of ritual has contributed vitally to the development of its symbolic form.[18] By the time of Germanus this new, Antiochene-style view of liturgy had begun to spin its allegorical web, not only at the entrances, but backwards and forwards into the rites that preceded and followed them.

One sees this verified above all in the "economic" interpretation of the Great Entrance as the funeral cortege of Jesus.[19] Here began a process whereby the whole liturgical action before and after the transfer of gifts was interpreted in function of the view that the gifts at the entrance represent the body of the already crucified Lord. This stimulated developments in the Prothesis or rite of preparation of the gifts at the beginning of the eucharist—especially the introduction of the prophetic "Suffering Servant" verses at the preparation of the eucharistic bread, thereby interpreting it as the sacrificial Lamb of God;[20] the solemnizing of the Great Entrance ritual itself and its symbolism; the resulting multiplication of burial-motif troparia at the deposition, incensing, and covering of the gifts on the altar, henceforth interpreted as representing the deposition of Jesus' crucified body in the sepulchre, its embalming with aromatic spices, and its wrapping in the winding sheet or sindon shroud. All this is indicative not only of the inevitable ritual elaboration of all medieval liturgies, but also of developments in piety and understanding. Here they not only interpreted existing text and ritual, but retroactively contributed to textual and ritual change.

A New Liturgical Book: The Diataxis

These developments, especially their almost riotous exaggeration in some medieval monastic manuscripts, eventually led to the appearance of a new liturgical book: the Diataxis or "order." This was a manual of rubrics describing just how the ritual was to be performed. By the tenth century we see the first inklings of a codification of rubrics among the Byzantines. In Italy these were often incorporated right into the liturgical text. In Constantinople and on Mt. Athos, separate manuals of rubrics began to multiply between the twelfth and the fifteenth centuries—especially to control exaggerated developments in the Prothesis rite. I shall say more about these Diataxeis at the end of the next chapter.[21]

Notes

1. Earlier (ch. 1, note 8), I avoided using this division of Byzantine history, but in this context it fits well enough for the period from Iconoclasm until the Latin Occupation.

2. I treat these issues in much greater detail in Taft, "Liturgy."

3. *Laudatio Marciani* 1, 47–72, R. Foerster, E. Richtsteig (eds.). *Choricii Gazaei opera* (Leipzig 1929) 78ff, cited in Mango, *Art* 32–3, 60–68. Another putative Palestinian witness attributed to John Damascene, is the discourse against iconoclastic emperor Constantine V Caballinus (741–775): *Adv. Constantinum Cabalinum*, PG 95:309–344; on church decoration, cf. chs. 3 and 10, PG 95:313–316, 325–328. This work was actually written by John of Jerusalem, synkellos of Patriarch Theodore of Antioch (750/51–773/74), ca. 764, and later revised in Constan-

tinople around 787. Cf. J. M. Hoeck, "Stand und Aufgaben der Damaskenos-Forschung," OCP 17 (1951) 26 note 2, citing B. M. Melioranskij, *Georgij Kiprijanin i Ioann Ierusalimljanin, dva malizvestnyx bortsa za pravoslavie v VIII veke* (St. Petersburg 1901). Schulz (52–54) discusses this document and cites in English translation the relevant passages.

4. *Homily 10, 6.* Trans. (slightly modified) from C. Mango, *The Homilies of Photius, Patriarch of Constantinople* (Cambridge, Mass. 1958) 186; id., *Art* 186. Formerly, this homily was considered to refer to the Nea or New Church inaugurated in 880 under Basil I. For its reassignment, see id. and R. J. H. Jenkins, "The Date and Significance of the Tenth Homily of Photius," DOP 9-10 (1955–1956) 123–140; Mango, *Art* 185.

5. Mango, *Art* 6, 13, 24, 57–60.

6. Ibid. 87, 89; cf. Mango, *Materials*, "Mosaics."

7. On the evolution of Middle-Byzantine church decoration, see especially J. Lafontaine-Dosogne, "L'évolution du programme décoratif des églises de 1071 à 1261," *Actes du XVe Congrès international d'Études byzantines, Athènes—Septembre 1976* (Athens 1979) I, 287–329 + planches XXVI–XXXIII; also O. Demus, *Byzantine Mosaic Decoration. Aspects of Monumental Art in Byzantium* (London 1948/New Rochelle, N.Y. 1976); O. Demus, E. Diez, *Byzantine Mosaics in Greece. Hosios Lucas and Daphni* (Cambridge, Mass. 1931); S. Dufrenne, *Les programmes iconographiques des églises byzantines de Mistra*, Bibliothèque des CA IV (Paris 1970); E. Giordani, "Das mittelbyzantinische Ausschmuckungssystem als Ausdruck eines hieratischen Bildprogramms," *Jahrbuch der österreichischen byzantinischen Gesellschaft* 1 (1951) 103–134; T. F. Mathews, "The Sequel to Nicaea II in Byzantine Church Decoration," *Perkins Journal* 41.3 (July 1988) 11–21.

8. PG 155:337-40.

9. Cf. the remarks of Mango, "Mosaics," 48.

10. It is said that the NT mysteries of salvation depicted are later standardized as the "Twelve Great Feasts," but that is only roughly true. In actual fact, one finds variety in the twelve mysteries actually depicted or listed as the "Great Feasts." Only ten are listed ca. 744 in John of Euboia, *Sermo in conceptionem S. Deiparae* 10, PG 96:1473C–1476A: the Annunciation (i.e., Conception) of Mary, her Nativity, the Annunciation of Gabriel, Jesus' Nativity, Hypapante, Epiphany, Transfiguration, Easter, Pentecost (I owe this reference to Dr. Alexander Kazhdan of Dumbarton Oaks Center for Byzantine Studies in Washington). The official liturgical list will eventually settle on the following twelve, given here in Byzantine calendar order: Nativity of Mary (Sept. 8), Exaltation of the Cross (Sept. 14), Entrance of Mary into the Temple (Nov. 21), Nativity of Jesus (Dec. 25), Theophany (Jan. 6), Hypapante (Feb. 2), Annunciation (March 25), En-

trance into Jerusalem (Palm Sunday), Ascension, Pentecost, Transfiguration (Aug. 6), Dormition (Aug. 15). The iconographic programs will also include the Resurrection (Easter), feast *hors pair* beyond all lists, and the Crucifixion (Good Friday), which is never listed liturgically among the Great Feasts.

11. Mango, "Mosaics," 48.

12. Mango, *Architecture* 197-8, and chapters 7-8 passim.

13. Mathews 144.

14. LEW 312.15-30 (right col.). On the provenance of this prayer, see Jacob, "Tradition," 117-118; id., "Zum Eisodosgebet der byzantinischen Chrysostomusliturgie des Vat. Barb. gr. 336," *Ostkirchliche Studien* 15 (1966) 35-38.

15. See T. F. Mathews, " 'Private' Liturgy in Byzantine Architecture: Toward a Reappraisal," CA 30 (1982) 125-138.

16. Cf. Taft, *Great Entrance* 178-94.

17. See my article "Sermon" in ODB 3:1880-1881.

18. On the history of this interplay of rite and interpretation in the Byzantine Rite, Schulz is especially good.

19. On this whole question, see Taft, *Great Entrance,* index p. 467 under "Great Entrance, symbolism: cortege and burial of Christ; id., "Liturgy," 53ff.

20. The history of the Prothesis is summarized in G. Descoeudres, *Die Pastophorien im syro-byzantinischen Osten. Eine Untersuchung zu architektur- und liturgiegeschichtlichen Problemen,* Schriften zur Geistesgeschichte des östlichen Europa, Bd. 16. (Wiesbaden 1983) ch. 6.

21. See Taft, "Mt. Athos," 192-194.

7 The Neo-Sabaitic Ascendancy

We have already noted that the monastic victory over Iconoclasm left the monks of Byzantium in an advantageous position vis-à-vis the secular clergy. The process of monasticization,
well underway before the Fourth Crusade (1204),[1] was height-
ened under Latin rule (1204–1261) when the demoralized secular clergy was unable to maintain the complex *Asmatike
Akolouthia* or "Sung Office" of the Great Church, and ac-
quiesced in the monasticization of the offices. During the
Paleologan restoration (1259–1453) the Byzantine Church remained a powerful force in the life of the people, especially
during the hesychast renaissance begun on Mt. Athos.[2] But
it was, henceforth, a Church under monastic leadership, not
only in its government and spiritual influence, but also in its
liturgical creativity.

From Studites to Hagiorites: The Rise of Mt. Athos

The early breakdown of Studite cenobitism and the rise of
Athonite or "hagiorite" monasticism were the key factors in
this evolution. In Constantinople, Studite cenobitism held its
own as the chief form of urban monasticism right into the thirteenth century. Elsewhere, however, the monastic center of
gravity had begun to move westward, as Turkish pressure in
the East shifted the focus of Byzantine monasticism from Asia
Minor to the monastic centers of Greece. The loss of Constantinople to the Latins from 1204–1261 was a severe blow to
Byzantine culture and society. But the vacuum left by the
weakening imperial power led to an increase in the prestige
and authority of the Church. Jurisdiction over Mt. Athos, for-

merly held by the emperor, was transferred to the patriarch in 1312, and monasticism continued to flourish in what was left of the rump "Empire of the Straits" in Europe.[3] This hagiorite monasticism, despite its Studite origins, eventually abandoned the strict cenobitism of the Studites for the more loosely structured Sabaitic monasticism of the lavras and sketes or small monasteries of Palestine.[4] Liturgically, at least, the same process was already underway in Constantinople itself. By the twelfth century, second-generation Sabaitic material had begun to infiltrate the offices of the Studite monasteries of the capital. This was the threshold of a new epoch, the final stage in the formation of today's Byzantine Rite.

The Neo-Sabaitic Synthesis

I call it "the neo-Sabaitic synthesis"—"neo" to distinguish it from the Studite Rite which, as noted in chapter 5, was an earlier synthesis of Sabaitic elements with the rite of Constantinople. That chapter outlined the long-standing liturgical interchange between Jerusalem and Constantinople, especially during the period of the Studite reform. This cross-fertilization intensified in the period following the disruption of hagiopolite liturgy through the destruction of the Jerusalem cathedral (the Basilica of the Anastasis or Holy Sepulchre as it is called in the West) by Caliph al-Hakim in 1009. From the eleventh century Palestinian monks reworked the Studite synthesis to suit their own needs. This was especially true with the order of night prayer (the agrypnia) and, later, the canon of daily orthros (matins) and the *pensum* of psalmody.[5]

The process was first described by Nikon of the Black Mountain (ca. 1025–after 1088), a monk of the Theotokos Monastery on the *Mauron Oros* north of Antioch in Syria. He was the first to use the word "typikon" for these new monastic ordinaries. In his spiritual testament prefacing his Typikon, he recounts:

> I came upon and collected different Typika, of Stoudios and of Jerusalem, and one did not agree with the other, neither Studite with another Studite one, nor Jerusalem ones with Jerusalem ones. And, greatly perplexed at this, I interrogated the

wise ones and the ancients, and those having knowledge of these matters and seasoned in things pertaining to the office of ecclesiarch and the rest, of the holy monastery of our holy father Sabas in Jerusalem, including the office of hegumen. . . .[6]

After informing himself about the "order (*taxis*) of the church and the psalmody," and on the various traditions oral and written, he adapted them for his own purposes (*Taktikon*, I). So, as the rite of Constantinople was being monasticized via Palestine, the rite of Palestine was being further Byzantinized. And although Nikon lists the differences between the usages of Stoudios and Jerusalem, a close reading of the *Taktikon* (I, 1–23) demonstrates that he is contrasting but two variants of basically the same Sabaitic rite. Both use the same Palestinian psalter of twenty kathismata[7]—they just distribute the *pensum* differently. At orthros both have *stichera* with lauds and *aposticha*[8]—but the hagiopolites omit the *stichera* on ferias. There are differences in the use of the Great Doxology (*Gloria in excelsis*) at orthros (I, 22), and the Studites do not say little (first) vespers before supper and great vespers after, as in the Palestinian agrypnia system.[9]

At the time of Nikon the only substantive difference between the usages was this *agrypnia*. The Sabaitic anchorites held an all-night vigil on the eve of Sundays and feasts, whereas the Studites adhered to the customary cenobitic horarium of evening prayer in sequential offices:

> It is necessary to know that . . . there is no agrypnia the whole night through, neither on feasts nor on Sunday, but rather the order of the ritual (*akolouthia*) at the time of apodeipnon [compline] and of mesonyktikon [midnight office] and of orthros [matins] according to the Typikon of Stoudios and of the Holy Mountain and, in a word, according to the custom of the cenobitic Diataxeis (*Taktikon* I, 20).

Further notable neo-Sabaitic developments included a considerable increase in the *pensum* of psalmody, and the daily nine-ode canon of orthros.[10] But it must be emphasized that both rites, Studite and neo-Sabaitic, are but variant usages of the same basic tradition.

Spread of the Typikon of St. Sabas

This neo-Sabaitic rite soon became popular everywhere. The reasons for this development are not altogether clear. Some guess it was because of its greater simplicity and less tightly-cenobitic style, in an age of decline and disarray, when the Great Church could no longer sustain the splendors of the old cathedral rite of Hagia Sophia, with its large number of singers,[11] and monasticism was less tightly disciplined than in the heyday of Studite cenobitism. Early in the twelfth century the essentially Studite Typikon of Evergetis,[12] one of the great cenobitic foundations of the capital,[13] already betrayed a large infiltration of neo-Sabaitic material into the Studite monasteries of Constantinople. Several other twelfth-century Typika borrowed heavily from the Evergetis Rule, and the Typikon of St. Sabas for the Serbian Monastery of Hilandar on Mt. Athos, which dates from ca. 1199, is little more than a Serbian version of it.[14] Later hagiorite Typika after the fifteenth century were all of the neo-Sabaitic tradition.[15] From Athos the new usage ultimately spread almost everywhere in the train of Athonite hesychasm.

Everywhere, that is, but Southern Italy. To give but one example, Dimitri Conomos notes during this period a fully monastic "flourishing Palaeologan musical renaissance"[16] which, like other post-Studite liturgical changes, found little support in Magna Graecia, where the older Asmatikon and Psaltikon repertories continued in use. This new movement was ultimately synthesized in the first half of the fourteenth century by a new composer, St. Ioannes Koukouzeles of the Great Lavra on Mt. Athos, on the eve of the hesychast ascendancy.[17]

Athonite Hesychasm Triumphant: The Diataxis of Philotheus

Especially influential in this diffusion of the new Sabaitic usages was the hagiorite hesychast Philotheus Kokkinos (d. 1379).[18] With the vindication of hesychast teaching, confirmed as official doctrine in the synods of 1347 and 1351, the hesychasts emerged as winners in a long struggle for hegemony in the

Orthodox Church and gained for their followers important positions in the hierarchy. Hesychast candidates controlled the Ecumenical Throne throughout the rest of the fourteenth century. The most celebrated among them was Philotheus, hegumen of the Great Lavra on Athos, bishop of Heraclea from 1347, and twice patriarch of Constantinople (1353–1355, 1364–1376). On his second accession to the patriarchal throne, Philotheus inaugurated a period of intense relations between the Phanar and the local Orthodox Churches beyond the Greek-speaking world. Along with the doctrinal, spiritual, and hierarchical dominance of the hesychasts, went liturgical influence. While abbot of the Great Lavra, Philotheus had composed two important liturgical ceremonials or Diataxeis: his *Diataxis tes hierodiakonias* for the Divine Office, and his *Diataxis tes Theias Leitourgias* for the eucharist. For all practical purposes, these Philothean rubrics still govern Byzantine liturgical celebration today. Studite-type manuscripts could still be found in use on Mt. Athos as late as the fourteenth century, before the Philothean reform, but in practically all fourteenth to sixteenth-century Greek codices the neo-Sabaitic arrangement canonized by Philotheus took over the field outside of Southern Italy and ultimately found its way into the first printed editions of the Byzantine liturgical books.[19]

Though these books were all published in Italy—chiefly in Venice, some in Rome—the earlier Studite office held its own in the monasteries of Southern Italy.[20] As for the eucharist, the first Italo-Greek edition, printed in Rome in 1601 for the use of Italo-Greek monks, still preserves at the Prothesis or preparation of the gifts before the liturgy, a local Calabrian rite far simpler than the Philothean ordo.

This is not surprising. Even in the monasteries of Mt. Athos, other Diataxeis continued to be composed and used in competition with the Philothean order right through the fifteenth century. It took even longer for the new usage to spread to the Byzantine Orthodox hinterlands beyond Greece and Constantinople: Slavonic manuscripts reflected the new order only after one or two centuries delay. But Philotheus' *Diataxis of the Divine Liturgy* was translated into Slavonic twice before the end of the fourteenth century,[21] and the neo-Sabaitic usage reached Rus' by the end of the fourteenth century, under Metropolitan Cyprian of Kiev (1381-2, 1390-1406), where it gradually replaced the old Studite use. The Trinity-Sergius Lavra north of Moscow adopted it in 1429; it took over Novgorod in 1441 and reached the northern extremity of Solovky on the White Sea by 1494.[22]

By the sixteenth century local usages had given way almost everywhere before the new system. By the seventeenth century the Venetian printed books were in general use, and the formative period of the Byzantine Rite as we know it had come to an end. The neo-Sabaitic usage in its fourteenth-century Athonite codification—basically the Rite of the Great Lavra during the abbacy of Philotheus—not only represents the triumph of hesychast monasticism over the urban Studite variety. If we except the local maintenance of the occasional Studite usage, especially in Southern Italy and Rus', it has also become the rite of world Orthodoxy. And it is what we know still as the "Byzantine Rite" today.

Notes

1. See Strunk, *Music* 137.
2. See Nicol, esp. ch. 2; J. Meyendorff, *St. Gregory Palamas and Orthodox Spirituality* (Crestwood, N.Y. 1974) 56-170; id., *A Study of Gregory Palamas* (London 1974), esp. part I. On the liturgical influence of the hesychast movement, see Taft, "Mt. Athos," 190-194.
3. See A. Kazhdan et alii, "Byzantium, History of," ODB I, 358-382.
4. I detail this evolution in "Mt. Athos."
5. Ibid.
6. *Preface* 9. V. N. Beneshevich (ed.), *Taktikon Nikona Chernogortsa: Grecheskij tekst po rukopisi No. 441 Sinajskago monastyrja sv. Ekateriny,* Vypusk I, Zapiski Ist.-Filol. Fakul'teta Petrogradskago Universiteta, chast' 139 (Petrograd 1917). References to the internal divisions of this document will be noted in the body of the text. See also id., *Opisanie grecheskix rukopisej Monastyrja sv. Ekateriny na Sinae* (St. Petersburg 1911) I, 561-601.

7. Divisions of the psalter comprising (ideally) nine psalms in three units of (ideally) three psalms each. On the Byzantine psalter traditions, see Taft, "Mt. Athos," 181-182.

8. Stichera and aposticha are poetic refrains repeated after verses of Sacred Scripture.

9. Taft, "Mt. Athos," 186-187.

10. Ibid. 188-190.

11. This is one of the reasons given by Symeon of Thessalonika (d. 1429), PG 155:553D, 625B.

12. Ed. Dmitrievskij I, 256-656. This huge liturgical customary is not contained in the new edition of G. Gautier, "Le Typicon de la Théotokos Evergétis," *Revue des études byzantines* 40 (1982) 5-101.

13. On the monastery, see R. Janin, *La géographie ecclésiastique de l'empire byzantin*, I.iii: *Les églises et les monastères* (Paris 1969) 178-84; J. Pargoire, "Constantinople. Le couvent (monastère) de l'Évergétis," *Echos d'orient* 9 (1906) 366-373; 10 (1907) 155-167, 259-263.

14. J. Thomas, "The *Evergetis* Monastery at Constantinople as a Center of Ecclesiastical Reform," Eleventh Annual Byzantine Studies Conference, *Abstract of Papers* (1985) 18.

15. M. Arranz, "Étapes," 67; id., "Matines," OCP 38 (1972) 86 note 1; id., "Les prières presbytérales de la 'Pannychis'," OCP 40 (1974) 331-2, cf. 342; id., "Hesperinos," 113 and note 20. As Arranz shows, earlier Athonite Typika reflect the Studite usage. Numerous neo-Sabaitic Typika are edited in Dmitrievskij III. On these documents, see also G. Bertonière, *The Historical Development of the Easter Vigil and Related Services in the Greek Church*, OCA 193 (1972) Part II.

16. Conomos, *Communion Cycle* 68.

17. Ibid. 68ff. On this composer see E. V. Williams, *John Koukouzeles' Reform of Byzantine Chanting for Great Vespers in the Fourteenth Century*, Yale University dissertation (Ann Arbor, Mich.: University Microfilms 1968); Strunk, *Music* 17ff and *passim* (see index p. 338); D. E. *Conomos*, "Koukouzeles, John," ODB 2:1155.

18. I tell the story in much greater detail, and with further references, in Taft, "Mt. Athos," 190-194.

19. Loc. cit., with further literature there.

20. As late as 1587 the Typikon of Grottaferrata, still in the Studite tradition, was adopted at St. Savior Monastery in Messina by order of Pope Sixtus V (Arranz, *Typicon* xxvii). Arranz, "Matines," OCP 38 (1972) 91 n. 2, on which I based my erroneous assertion in Taft, "Mt. Athos," 192, would lead one to believe (incorrectly) that this represented a shift to the Sabaitic Typikon. I am grateful to my student, S. Parenti, for pointing out my error.

21. Taft, "Mt. Athos," 193 and n. 120.

22. Arranz, "Étapes," 70-72.